[MUTATION : SELECTION]

DEEP SURVIVAL

RYAN MORROW

POETRY

Acknowledgments

A special thank you to both Summer Rose and Mitch Green for letting me use and abuse their artistic prowess. It's not always easy dealing with the demands of a madman. The vision of "Deep Survival" would not have been possible without either of you. I am lucky to have access to your talents and you've both made this book an extremely superb work of art.

Summer Rose created, and hand drew all the interior drawings excluding the center splash page.

Mitch Green designed the cover, the center splash page, and overall typograph of the book.

NOTE FROM AUTHOR

I think it was Camus that said, "In order to understand the world, one has to turn away from it on occasion." Actually, I know the great Albert Camus said this, because we have the omnipotent Google to verify such claims. This particular statement by him seemed fitting for a brief description of what "Deep Survival" is about, as much as anything can be about something anyway. And much like Sisyphus or really any of us, if we are to find "meaning" in anything at all we must accept the absurd. Any and all human acts hold equal potential to be meaningless or fulfilling, we create the value of all our treasures. But certainly, no treasure can be worth anything without a journey and not without strife. In this vain, I have polished a few of my stone words, rolled them up an infinite incline, and will be dropping them into the beautiful abyss of your eyes. I hope with no expectations, that all of you will enjoy it somehow. In stores Spring 2018. Thanks for reading.

XXXXX Ryan Morrow XXXXX

This book is dedicated to a nuance. a certain shade. an impossible hue. the difference. and everything almost in-between.

It isn't often that you can find a brother in arms within this community. It also isn't often that you can be absolutely humbled by the force of his talent and drive. Morrow and I met this way...by making shit happen. It started off with a few phone calls and then flourished into a couple of maniacs spewing ideas from every orifice possible. Then it was an impromptu visit where we bled and sang together late into the feverish night. He writes in a way that I cannot begin to fathom. An execution of cunning tongue in cheek, and intellect that is rare these days in the age of the one liners. A delight to read, consume, and shit out while you are hungover from pure mental drunkenness. Reading his work has been such a delight to the senses and to be honest at times, a mind fuck. But that is always how it should be. True artists like Morrow make you rethink your own game, make you change your stride, make you look at yourself in the mirror with a new set of bloodshot eyes. This and many more of his collections will always be his finest work. He is not done yet, dear readers.

In love and terror,
Matt Baker

"IT IS BY GOING DOWN INTO THE ABYSS THAT WE RECOVER THE TREASURES OF LIFE. WHERE YOU STUMBLE, THERE LIES YOUR TREASURE."

- JOSEPH CAMPBELL -

A
S
C
E
N
S
I
O
N

CROWNED PAWNS

So far from home
yet as safe as a baby
in the primordial womb

Torn from reality
yet all the while - tasting every moment
as if nothing else existed

Unable to be distracted -
for there is nothing left
to distract from

I am the lord of my silence
The king in a realm of one
Mastering an art
no one else can decipher

The painter
and the canvas
have united

The sculptor
removes only
pieces of himself

The writer
forges new words
just to take his next breath

DAMNED TO BLISS

As I caress the long fragile spine
of this ever hungry moment -
I am crushed
by its commanding beauty

Its demand of both tears
and the howl of excess -
keeping my hopes hidden like broken feathers
on the wings of fallen angels

I am damned to this bliss
accommodating my soul – for a cataclysm
Seeds like bombs in the virgin womb
of an eager universe

I ONLY CAME HERE FOR THE BOOZE

They want to know things - about me
I just give them the finger
They drag their fat bodies across the room
to ask me about my weekend
I lie to them, and say "not much"
They look over at me - then look away
I try and light them on fire with my mind
They try and blackmail me with their goofy smiles
I just keep drinking...

They want to tell me - about their shitty wives
and preposterously depressing lives
their vacation plans to Nebraska
their lame new American made cars
the RV's
the TV's
the me me me's

They want to know
what *"I think"*
about this or that politician – some decaying celebrity
about fucking S.P.O.R.T.S.
"Listen man...., I don't give a good god damn!"

They try and give me advice
I never asked for
I look them up and down
and let out a good hard laugh
I just keep drinking...

A LATE THANK YOU LETTER

Just when I was convinced
that every face in the crowd
was merging into one big scowl -
staring right at me
like a rotting piece of flesh
on their china white plates

Just when I think
my anxiety might manifest itself
into a giant ball of fire -
a faceless stranger
does the only thing left
to tip the scales

They turn in my lost wallet
And at a horse track no less!
They don't slip out a 20 spot
for themselves
They don't try running
any of the shiny cards -
not even for a single beer

They turn it in -
with all its desperate contents
still fully intact
They don't want a thank you letter
they just do the right thing
and move along

Just when I was convinced
it was all flatlines and revenge
floating around in tight little skulls
Just when I thought I was betting on doom itself
one lights up and destroys the darkness

Even thou I got just as drunk that day -
as any other day
Even thou I spent every bit of money I had -
in my resurrected wallet
Even thou Dean Butler let me down -
in all six races
I still strolled out of the track that day
one hell of a winner

A STORY IN THE SKY

"Those were the days"
of course you never know that
when you're in them -
but they were

Sitting there like new age philosophers
15 stories up on a room in the clouds
15 stories into a dream within a dream
A condominium fit for a king
or maybe just two simple beggars
Calhoun Lake far below - in all its subtle brilliance
reflecting back into our young introspective eyes
Cross-legged on the floor
we twisted the world around in our heads
and passed our strange creations
back and forth to each-other's wet brains

over hot tea
over cold beer
over red wine
over dry gin
and most importantly
over many a game of 'tigers and goats'
This always seemed odd to me -
Because they appear to be the obvious choice
Being such supreme predators and all
But the goats I guess - they always have each other
I'm still convinced
that the tigers can never really win

Way down below us
on those cool Uptown streets
the woman just passing us by
All dressed to kill -
any man they encountered

Packs of beautiful ladies below
in long single file lines
heading to clubs, to dive bars
to broken hearts and hazy memories
to endlessly tell men, "No thank you"
and "I don't think so" and "just move along buddy"
so on and so forth

But to Hell with them we said
because that was our time and
those were our days
where the woman came as an afterthought
to the kingdom -
growing in our minds

We were tucked away
safely in our castle in the sky
where the world was just a brain game
and the woman - just tiny dots below

A WAY TO KNOW ITSELF

The Universe
is a
vehicle
and our hearts
grip the
keys

The Cosmos
is the
paint
and our minds
are its finest
brush

The World
is a
weight
and our hands
balance the
scales

A WRINKLE IN SPACE-TIME

A pocked and worn face - floats effortlessly and stoic
above the wreckage of a thousand memories

Unable to be convinced - it can no longer act surprised
It only waits for what it knows belongs

The fleeting spasms of pain - are but expected
annoyances of its meditation

The persistent throb of desire is but
the metronome – of an ancient beat still beating

Everything is now so overwhelmingly beautiful -
that it blacks out the sky

A deep trance found like slow harmony -
drowning out everything else

The face salivates only for destruction -
Dripping in waves down the curves of apocalypse

This eternal season must be penetrated-
A plea for winter when the flowers burn like mad suns

There is no ceiling - but there must surely
be a bottom to this spiral

ALL NIGHTMARES START AS DREAMS

If you were given ten tries
you would still beg for ten more

If they granted you three wishes
you would wish for three more

If you received a thousand nights
you would still desire just one more

ALL TOGETHER NOW

We're all lost in the twisted maze
We're all ship-wrecked
and nearly helpless
imperfect - broken - mad
We travel through space locked in a death orbit
Spinning around an insane king made of fire
It's reign is pure in all its chemical precision
unquestionable - unforgiving - narcissistic
We are all slightly confused
conflicted fools
tap-dancing hypocrites
doomed beggars - soiled by guilt
Sealed in island vessels
Peering from behind two filthy windows
Inside a shifting house that began collapsing
just as soon as it was constructed
We are buried inside ourselves
unable to understand ourselves
We are all variables in an equation with no answer
The only thing left that cannot be reduced -
is to have a bit of style
Style is the human constant
The style of our suffering - is everything
The art of dying - with some class
We must get as intoxicated as we can
shouting into the void, "Fuck off, you bastards!"
with all the charisma we can muster

ANCIENT SOIL , NEW LOAM

Excavating history
to feed the future gardens -
wealth in organic remains

black and heavy
weighted and deep -
rich manifold universe

Is it not the greatest magic trick of all?
That from rotting decay comes more life.

One insestual language
consuming and regurgitating -
four letters to shape it all

Freeing the elements
from biochemical chains -
feeding the codex

Information downloaded
into cellular machinery -
consciousness flips on

Within every grave
is the opportunity -
to live again

O M N I

I create things
just to have the opportunity
to destroy my own creation

I destroy things
so I am not as simple as I appear

I create things
so I am not trapped inside a limited frame

I destroy things
to show you I can escape the maze I define

I create things
in order to feel not so minuscule
irrelevant
insignificant

I destroy things
to feel powerful
arrogant
insane

I create things
in order to expand myself

I destroy things
to disappear

I use art to procreate
my everything

I destroy art
to radiate my nothing

THE PILGRIM

I allow the long slender fingers
of her glorious hell
to slide deep into
my heart

I am destroyed
with every kiss
recreated
in the next

I am but a pilgrim
content to wander
her unforgiving wilderness
for an eternity

THE MASK OF HUMANITY

We are all chaos
wearing the mask
of humanity

You
me
and infinity

We are just agents
of the stars -
cosmic reservoir dogs

one big circle of life and death
a cosmic gun -
against each of our skulls

We are all simply survival
in the skin
of an identity

You
me
and infinity

We are just excited particles
smashing together
like cosmic perverts

In one big universal circle jerk
shooting phallic light streams
into each-other's blackholes

ASCEND TO HELL

only in the deepest of abyss
are we driven toward true light

transcending downward
ascending to hell

We are gods unable to control
the fire in our hearts

The only art we understand
is made by destruction

ephemeral masterpieces
cosmic powder kegs

COSMIC CHILDREN

We are born
into a world we cannot control
yet we still try
O' but for the glory - we try
struggling against profound currents
swallowing the smallest of trivialities
hanging them up as victories

We are air dropped
into the center of a vast desert
doomed to the searching
yet we crawl on
knowing full well
that every shifting paradise
is a vapor ghost
disintegrating
just as soon as we make contact

We weep when we're happy
and weep in total sadness

We laugh when finding humor
and laugh in total madness

Conflicted
contradicting
paradox

FOR WHAT IT'S WORTH

So far no one can live forever -
tragically many hardly live at all
war, disease, and circumstance
pull the strings of our fate

So sometime I like to just stop
and take in a long deep breath
and scream into the sky
"I am a fucking survivor! "
"I'm alive!"
because for what it's worth
in that moment it's true
Sometimes I like to just start running
as fast as I possibly can
deep into the woods as
if chased by the flames of hell -
And I seem to float like an angel
falling past the clouds

It's not arrogance nor strength
that remains in me
but rather an immovable humbleness
and an irresistible awareness
Pride is just a children's game
we play in Earth's sandbox
Tomorrow may bring
the long silence to my tongue
and a flatline to my heart -
but I am no longer afraid
This time was always borrowed -
with no interest
or repayment plan
It's just the universe counting itself
For me that has always been
payment in itself

FLOWERS GONE MAD

She surprises me
with each step

Every moment
an immaculate gift

My eyes tear open
with uncontrollable elation

Her beauty is blooming
like a flower gone mad

She fills my every niche
with the color of bliss

My skin impenetrable armor
set in place with her kiss

The world's problems
now bend like straw

useless and weak
against my swollen chest

JUST LISTEN

Baby - don't mind all those other boys
they just want to play you -
play all your singles
on repeat

play them when it's convenient
and then toss your sweet music
in the fifty-cent bin

I want the whole package
the deluxe
the liner notes
and even the little stickers

Once that needle hits
we're sitting through
the whole damn thing

the loud stuff
the soft parts
the solos
the epic outro

I'll cherish the album
in its entirety baby

In the land of radio Tourette's
I'll be the medicine

In this zoo of shuffle crazy maniacs
I'll be the audiophile in the wild

OPAQUE EYES

Opaque eyes
indestructible lies
withered hearts
rusted parts
unconscious masses
one way looking glasses

The hordes grow
radiated strange glow
mutant horrors
death explorers
twisted fiends
hell crafted machines

Intoxicated mad
eternal nomad
delusional might
devoid of all light
tortured immortal
demonic cabal

Summon shapes
impossible landscapes
imbue the abyss
capture dark bliss
all the power
loneliest tower

THE PARADISE OF DELIRIUM

There are things you
shall never understand
Such beautiful moments
dressed in the most
hideous of circumstance

There are maidens
of unbearable light
inside caskets
you're too afraid
to ever peer inside

You must kiss death
to know death
You must court disaster
to truly dance
You must eat of the poison apple
to feel absolute love

There is an alien spaceship
in the center of our minds
ready to transport us
to the furthest limits
of our desire
All we have to do is say, "Yes"
to their divine abduction
Ween ourselves from
our innate mother's milk

Fear is the last sentry
guarding the gates
to the paradise of delirium

NERVOUS SMILE

I put in the hours
it's an ok job
I got my freedoms
It pays well enough
if I get diarrhea
I can skip a day or two
and nobody seems to mind
The depression
can be kept at bay

I come home
It's a nice house
It's got its perks
the toilet works
the furnace blows hot air
the big yard is nice
a place for the dog to run wild

I have a cool dog
the dog is cute
the dog listens most of the time
the dog's a real pal
she fetches
she plays
she shits in a designated area
I have a girlfriend
my girlfriend's really great
she's gorgeous
she laughs a lot
she drinks and
she's fun as hell
she's fantastic in bed
o' yeah she also despises
sports and politics

I have nervous hands
that hold all these luxuries
I have an anxious mind
a mind that sees a flood
a mind that starts fires
a mind that rarely sleeps
a mind like a paranoid ruler
a mind that thinks all my nice things
can't possibly last much longer

THE PURSUIT

Chase
the story
not the thrill

Charm
the snake
devour the kill

AS WE DISCOVER IT

I am a particle
drifting
in your spaces
a drifter seeking
always
for his queen

I am a comet
sailing
forever in your expanses
a sailor
that no longer needs
a compass

I am a seed
planted
in your infinite soil
a flower
that can't stop
blooming

I am a poet
drowning
in the depths
of your inkwell
destined
to find the bottom

I am an astronaut
and you are my spacecraft
together
we create
the universe
as we discover it

GODS OF FERTILITY

These words are weapons
in this war of attraction

These words are bricks
and I build my fortress to secret skies

These words are crushed velvet
when everything is thorns

hidden power when
everything seems weak

These words - they see things
invisible to the dragon's eyes

These words are renegades
stomping through the stiff pages of complacency

A rising howl
refusing to be silenced

These words are armor
resisting the world's attack
These words are a vehicle
to anywhere we can imagine
Advanced technology
the limits of which remain unknown

These words are
the new gods of fertility
mushrooming
multiplying
spawning
insane with desire

These words are
indestructible

Our dreams gone mad
and climbing out of reality

Stories breed more stories
The myths beget themselves

amphibious changelings
all the way down

Mobius strips
all the way around

endless and pure
they can't be uncreated

These words are proof
that the mind approaches infinity

A HIGHWAY NAMED DESIRE

We're driving down the interstate of our desires
and we can't slow down

There is a glorious constant beauty
streaming past our peripheries

We are flying like bullets made of bliss
taking the fastest route to satisfaction

We won't be on this ride for long
but if I've done the math correctly

I think we both have
just enough time to get off!

AND SO IT GOES

And so we go to war -
once more
battling our fears
conquering the pain

Each day
there is a new army
to replace the old

We're not brave
and we're not strong
But we can still hold our own

Wearing our scars
with bloodied pride
every day - taking back
a piece of our kingdom

The severed heads
of all our victories
growing ever more bodies

Our stubborn hearts
finding ever more ways
to beat to the chaos

REPEAT

I can only
be washed
of this poison

by bathing
in new
intoxications

TRUE COLOR OF THE FLAME

I shall burn through this paper
as I burned through our time together
ruthless, free, and unafraid

I pull another moment from the stack
I load laughter and love
into this greedy machine

I exhaust my pain in droves
but only beautiful music exits
singing us away

They can't possibly understand
the true color of these flames
when not in the center of the fire

They will never grasp
the strength of these temptations
that I cannot resist

CHEMICAL ADVICE

"You must promise me one thing"
he said
as the last of the leaves
fell from his skull
"Plant at least one seed every day"

HELLION

His name was Sundance

and he was a class A sinner
with charisma in hordes

He talked his way out of everything
and in to every bedroom

His smile bent bullets
right around his skull

A tongue quicker
than a Texas viper

and on the tip - something
far worse than common poison

His eyes were a calm abyss
something to stare at
with no center

Sundance never asked for much
he just took what he needed
and made that the new way

He only like the good times
and never really cared for the rest
When the blood was really flowing
he was at peace

When the drugs were worth a damn
he was an army
And when there was a beautiful woman
his heart knew no limits

He made the world unfold
creating bliss from devastation

There was Hell to be had
And he had it all dancing –
in the palm of his hand

PERSIG

The discipline
to let it go

The wisdom
to watch it burn

The strength
to stay silent

The knowledge
to play no card at all

The chance
to understand
the truth of Quality

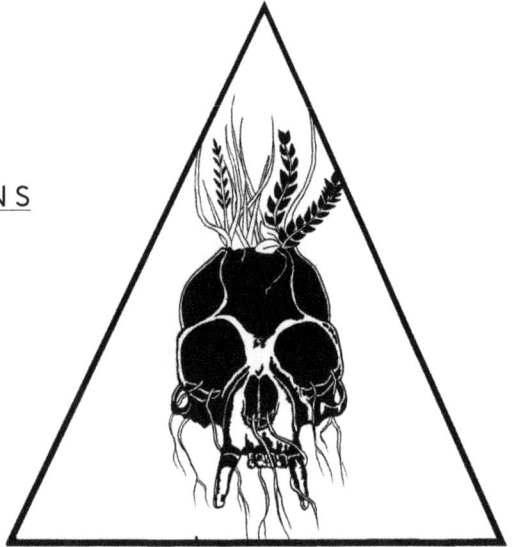

DECOMPOSITIONS

constant death
is the
secret ingredient
for the
richest soil

APPRECIATION

In-between sips
of the most decent wine
a "lower-middle" class man
can afford
Behind warm
comfortable walls
A refrigerator full
of un-hunted meats
and un-gathered fruits
easy calories
Three paces from
a gallon of processed ice cream
A bank account in the green
An insurance plan
no wife
no x-wives
no kids
no debts
just Healthy American Blood
No natural predators
No STDs
No phobias
No psychosis
A solid education
Important documents
spilling out from
solid oak filing cabinets
A little black book
filled with pretty names
New kicks
A fresh drink in hand
stereo system cranked
the night is so young –
so desperately young

YOU ASKED ME WHAT THE DIFFERENCE IS

Listen man -
I know what you're saying but
I need to write my poetry on the road
in the moment
on bar napkins
on flesh
with crayons
on ecstasy
in basements
with strangers
I need the rush of despair
I feed on the secrets
the mystery
each word - its own destiny

Will it get lost in my pocket?
soaked in the wash?
or swim effortlessly away in the rain?
Will it drift into obscurity?
be forgotten?
scribbled over?
torn to shreds?

You write
in a cubicle of safety
you type motivational words
in fancy fonts
with the hopes they will
inspire and encourage
I write
because I must

Listen man -
I need my poetry to really cut
like a weapon
thrown with killing intent
Not darts
thrown at a scoreboard

My poems are violent regurgitations
vomiting up the depths of me
into a harsh sunlight
Your poems are just lugi's
hacked up phlegm balls
empty love letters
spit out
to nobody at all

DEAD ASTRONAUTS

I'm a non-believer
and the only way
to change my mind
is to take me
to your leader

DEATH WISH

In pain
we taste
purpose

In bliss
we sip
oblivion

And in between
are all the flavors
of our death-wish

TIME IS A SCAR

When you've heard
this many gunshots
you're ready for war
and shy all at the same time

When you've been cut
this many times
the knifes are all useless
and terribly dull

When you've lived
this many lives
It's no longer about god
or his devil

MOLECULE

The nectar
never leaves
my tongue

It lingers
like a snake
within the garden

dragging
like an anchor
upon the sea floor

Hibernating
like a mighty bear
inside the proverbial cave

And all
within
a moment

the loveliest
of
destructions

the most
serene
of intoxication

pulled into action
by the command
of divine hunger

I would taste
a world of
bitter fruit

I would eat a
universe
of spoiled seed

for just one more
molecule
of her sweet flower

CLIPPED

Can you feel that?
It is the zenith
of foreign pleasure
It's the first climax
with a woman full of love
It's a perfectly ripe fruit
in a desolate place

Can you see it now?
It's there on the horizon
It's waiting for us to arrive
with story and verse
It's a hollow thing that needs us
to make it whole again

Pay the reapers no mind
Don't let the heat slow your stride
Nor this impossible weight
pull you from your wave
If any of this were easy
we would all be lunatics by now

These words are just scars
carved into the paper
proof that we're alive
they mark us as we mark them
A war of mutual attrition
Our time flows like ink
the blood dries
and the story remains

Can you feel that?
That's the delight
of a life worth living
O' the stories they shall tell!
Around the proverbial campfire
we laugh and dance
wild animals set loose upon the cosmos

These words protect our hearts
The poetry armors our minds

Fearless of what's to come
we are determined ghosts
still haunting the earth
by shear curiosity
invincible to shame
and eternally the fool
we seduce the angels themselves
to clip their wings and fall

INFINITE BOTH WAYS

I want it all
and I want it now
yet you could take everything
and I couldn't care less

I'll kill to be king
yet I crave to be the beggar
all in the same instant
I am everything and nothing

I will dine in your master's-chamber
I will maniacally bathe in liquid gold
and then I shall walk into the streets
cover myself in all the filth I can find

I will sit in the desperate black
with no hope to escape
Give me cosmic orgasms
followed by incredible injury

The hourglass is too deceptive
the sand - just a billion tiny liars
Time is a twisted chameleon
with infinite colors

Happiness is an executioner
that kills you with its love
The heart is a *Matryoshka* doll
infinite both ways

We grow
only to decay
Always all the time
and never once

HEARTSTRINGS

There is a string
pulled between
our hearts –

Every night
I
dance

with the grace
of a
drunken monkey

from one side
to the
other

INSPIRE / EXPIRE

Inspiration lies in folded form
in twisted masks
and dull colors

Cast off the search
for that which
must find you

Victims to a shadowed stalker
lurking in the perimeter
of our own mind

Without our control
hearts held hostage
at pen-point

Pulling our shaking hands
into the gears
of the typewriter

Seduce the breaking
of our hearts
for all their black ink

Inspiration's gold
is not asked for -
nor payed for

A desperate lover
waiting in the cracks of a moment
like a slumbering dragon

A cunning killer
ready to deliver us from oblivion
and show us a new way

Vivid dreams disintegrate
intoxication fades
Sleep is a tiny death

DARK MATTER IS THE TEARS OF THE UNIVERSE

My consciousness is cracked
I barely know a *thing* at all

I survive on nothing more than broken imagery
- a sense of yearning despair

I'm drifting inside a blackened mirror
I float, therefor I must exist - right?

I squeeze the life from everything beautiful
just so I know it's mine

My mind is fractured
I barely remember a *thing* at all

I survive for the pure joy of suffering
and a deep romanticism for doom

I get exactly what I deserve
because I don't need a *thing* at all

I am pulled in a billion scattered directions
in simultaneous symphony

I absorb the universe into my void
I will never die alone!

ODE TO SLOW MADNESS

Jazz and a stiff drink
cause it never gets easier -
just a little easier to handle
with the right finesse

So little in the way of
Eureka's! and Violas!
More of a slow grind to
small victories
More of a long cool blues solo
than the dropping of a techno beat

Waltzing through life
with a nervous and unpredictable
dance partner
just trying to keep the beat

Jazz and a glass of red wine
cause it rarely makes more sense
than it does right now

So rare for us to find
what we're looking for
Mostly lonely nights pondering why
and then when

Sifting through the shit of life
to find a few more jigsaw pieces
to an impossibly huge puzzle
You can make out the image of something
but it never has context

Jazz and surrender
cause the realest hack of life
is learning to enjoy the suffering

CHESHIRE CAT

There is a fixation
with the pain
encased within
her kiss

A quiet killer
slithering
in the rim
of her light

A face in the
shadow
Grinning like
The Cheshire Cat
It knows something
that I will never
be allowed
to understand

Yet I thrive
off that twisted harvest
her passion rations
to my feeble urges

I stumble off every cliff
I dance on the hottest coals
I bury myself in my own grave
with the illusion
that it all meant something....
just to make her smile

HOWLING AT DEAD STARS

Wild is my heart
strange is my love

A powerful thirst
in every drop
of my blood

If you ever get
close enough
to see the fire in
my eyes

I promise
you won't leave -
without a mark

PEEPING TOM

Here I sit on pulverized stones
looking up the yearning stems
of two bowed palm trees

Nothing could distract me
as I gaze up the legs
of nature's skirt

From the barrel of my eye
into the heart of an
endless summer

I give my very life
to taste what's between
earth's thighs

JINN AND TONIC

When we make love
we are but
two genies
rubbing
each other's lamps
granting
infinite wishes

PAIN AS CURRENCY

You can't possibly expect
to run through
the barbed wire
and not become scared

There is no respect
for a crown inherited
without knowing the war
that created it

There is no honor
blindly following
bloodless hands
commanding invisible armies

I'll gladly sacrifice security
for the prize of a hero's journey
Inspiration comes at the cost
of a simple life

FOREIGN TONGUE

I'm here to eat
the most exotic of fruit

I'm here to let the waters
cleanse the deepest of stains

I'm here to be humbled and awed
to single points in a vast masterpiece

True wisdom is knowing when to swing the hammer
and when to put it down

True knowledge is understanding
how the hammer got there

I'm here to preserve myself
in the amber of these moments

I hold perfectly still
while the jungle cyclically breathes

life and death in hot waves
cascading through symbiotic inhabitants

Healing infinite tiny cuts
all the while consuming itself
just to stay alive

REFLECTION / REFRACTION

There is a stranger in my bed
and it's getting stranger every night
There is a stranger in my head
and it's beginning to freak me out
There's a strange man occupying the mirror
doing the things that I used to do
The less I pay attention
the more the menace grows
I try my damnedest to
go about my day
pretending I can't see the faces that it makes
the risks that it's taking
I wear jet black sunglasses
in hopes it doesn't notice me
I hide behind thick wooden doors
just to avoid the chance...
I can be found
hunched over a typewriter
for hours at a time
but the stranger is there as well
glaring
judging
taunting
whispering things in my ears
and putting that tickle
in my guts
I'm starting to want
the things that it wants
see things
just the way it see things
It's starting to seem
a little less strange
and a little more like change

ROYAL JELLY

Here we go again
her glorious frame
arched and howling
for my hands to engage

Her eyes tell me
everything
I need to know -
the garden is blooming

My tongue is the means
of extraction

Every fruit must be tasted -
for tonight
is the harvest
Before the sun
brings extinction

I am the brute
that deserves nothing
the maniac
set loose into the streets -
into her wilderness

But she doesn't mind
my crazy stare
She doesn't stop me
when I can't stop myself

Here we go again
our lips burning from the friction
in an attempt
to fuse our lust
Her eyes are traps
but once inside
I dare not escape

Her eyes are traps
but once inside
I won't want to escape

The garden is blooming
out of control
One tongue
could never keep up
with her fountain of nectar

BLACKHOLE PROPHET

I no longer need the frills
the extras
or the side dish

I want the meat on the bone
I want the stuff raw

label me intense
call me absurd
call me when you're bored

but I no longer feel your guilt
or understand your crippling circumstance

I no longer see the colors you see
I dream in shades of white fire
I grip what you're too afraid to touch

I risk the days blazing sun
and survive into the sanctum of night

unabashed and righteous
My eyes need more nightmares – more fuel

unsustainable and glorious
Destructive but purely creative

I'm enlightened in the furthest depths
of expanding seas

I'm dead in outer space
holding a perfect smile

galaxies rises and fall in me
fragments of the universe exploded within me

I am spinning with the mad intent
of a banished deity

The mouth of chaos will always
accommodate my fleshy fury

Bent beyond repair
Mangled into rebirth

O' blackhole prophet
gaze upon my sacrifice

MYTHMAKER

We can't wait for it -
gritting teeth and
biting tongues

We won't stand for it -
clawing walls and
tearing hearts

the shadow of a man
is dancing
in distant bliss

the lust in our eyes
could drown
the kingdom

the desire in us
will reinvent
their fire

Our love is a fallen angel
flying back
to heaven

death's caress
is tender
as it peels back reality

the sweet taste
of fear in
beautiful abyss

We burn
like all
dead gods do

VANITY IS A VAMPIRE

He speaks as if his words were potent
As if behind his lips were a weapon
Believing the scales of fate to feel his weight
Tied up within an impossible knot he squirms with pride

Convulsing to erratic drumbeats and naming it art
With a world filled with such interesting temptations
he never once thought to just close his eyes
The illusion of self is as palpable as blood is red

He dines in halls of golden perfection
feasting in excess on hollow sustenance
He thirsts forever for his own missing reflection

UNCOIL

When I am at my most complex
knotted up and twisted round
some long forgotten meaning

That's when she appears -
My mathematician
of desires

unlocking all my doors
with the flick of her wrists

untangling all my fears
with such delicate fists

sorting all the oblong pieces
into dazzling geometry

Solving the Rubik's Cube
within my chest

with the batting of her eyes
There is nothing left to decide

all doubt crumbles
under love's logic

I am The Coiled One
She is an infinite sky

STAINED-GLASS

A shattered heart
never gets put back together
quite the way it started

if you're lucky enough
to have it destroyed
a second time

It might be wise
to just get used to
all the pretty pieces

SKIN DEEP

I was the man
without a face
unrecognizable
to myself
'for I never
left the stage

I was a man
with a thousand
dead ends
but not one
way through

I was a brilliant
astronaut
stranded in
space on a ship
with no fuel

I was a circus
chimpanzee
competing in a
spelling bee

I have become
the Renaissance Man
of every dive bar
in this sunken city

I'm a legend
in some
ripped up
children's book

I was the man
without a face -
but I shall
carve a new one
from the skin
of future's past

COFFIN / VASE

I am a grave
and she is
the beautiful flower
that blooms
out from me

I am all but forgotten
and she is
the resilient thing
that finds a way
through

EAT TO SURFACE

Inside
the belly
of despair

Lost
and
driven
mad

Sick -
with the
virus
of life

I do not
intend
to eat
to the surface

until I have
consumed
the hearts
of all my beasts

MIRROR-MASK

There is
no man
beneath
this
mask
only a
mirror
reflecting
an ever changing
face

THE DEEP CARESS

Wet brains - yearning heart
Open wounds - bloodstained art
Walking - stalking twisted path
feet calloused - a mind of wraith

Up above - torn apart
blackened skies
On the wire - in the bleak
abysmal eyes

Tired hands - broken grip
Old scars - permanent fat lip
Shifting - sifting junkyard man
Wandering star - wasteland artisan

Just above - descending down
winged darkness
Occult spell - woven words
surrender to the deep caress

THE ONES THAT CAME BEFORE

The poetry of the dead
is amplified -
through the dirt
and the years

each word sharpening
in the moon's
reflective grin

necrotic power
sacrosanct
forever unbreakable

eternal wisdom
echoes from
the ones who came before

so wild in their stillness
so defiant
in their halcyon pages

unable to be devoured
by our
carnivorous hands

their beauty
now entombed
in utopian shades

I can only unfurl my mind
and hope some of their insight
seeps into my folds

SHUFFLE

All our
perceived
order -
is but
a single day
in the life
of chaos

THANATOS

I am transposed from below
I am Thanatos climbing

I was baptized in fire
but those flames have subdued

In a blazing crown of grandeur
all my fear became gold

I am now a mere mortal
reborn from these trials

I seek only true love
from every soul that I encounter

I demand the very best
of all who dare seek my light

NOW WE BEGIN

Ah, now we can truly begin
A few drinks down
a couple nights in

Sweating out the poison
of the civilized man

Dissipating the smog of fear
miasma of trivialities
pounding flood of I's & O's

They are all parting now
like the borders of a drastic cut
to reveal the meat within

In this place
all nutrition is provided
nothing really dies
and nothing shall go to waste

every scrap recycled
into the heart of youth
all value preserved
in humming valances

Everything moving
like blades through vacancies

ecstasy is as easy
as the first breath
Truth much easier

Unburdened we ascend
cerebral mountain bend
ants in space – without end

THE LIBRARIANS

We are each-other's librarians
stacking memories
just like old books
in an infinite library

SEASON OF SURRENDER

It is the sweetest torture
that I have ever known
To hold her body
like a dying fire
in a frozen world

In the final hours
before the twilight
Where the moon still casts
its voyeuristic eye
on our brief paradise

My hands find her hips
with the tenacious courage
of a holy pilgrim
Each pass across her lands
there is something new to discover

My lips invade
her slumbering valleys
bringing the promise
of future rains
to honor her lush and sacred habitats

The engagement is
always fleeting
doomed to end
But just as exquisite
as the rose that wilts
upon the zenith of its glory

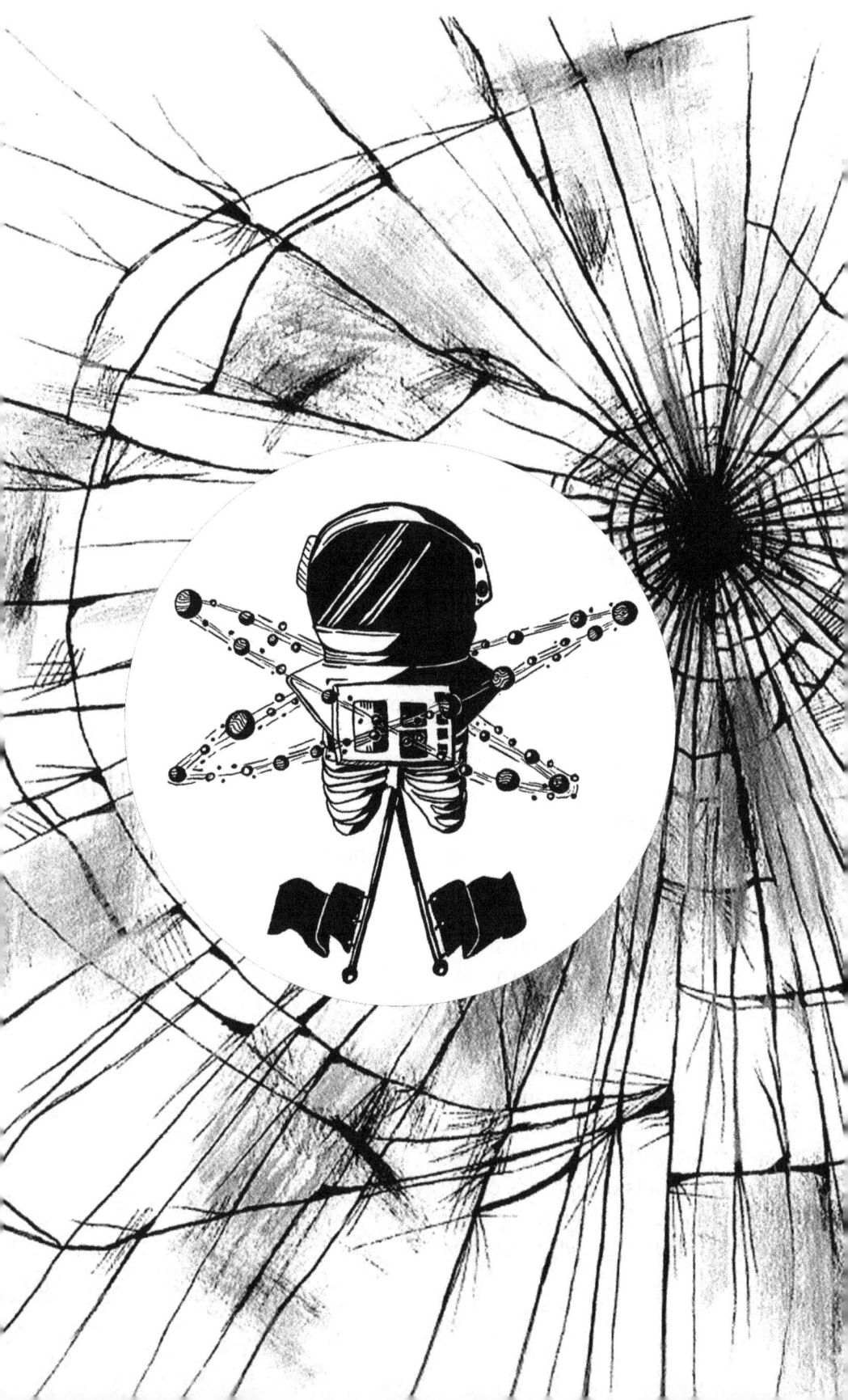

INTERNAL SPACESHIPS

Craving the mysteries
howling for deeper awe
Like a curious cat
drawn into the darkness
of the mind's alleyways
Compelled
to hunt moments
yet unable - to be seen

Too many of our poets -
are destroyers
Collapsing glorious anomalies
into ever simple
and fragile emotions
They drag our best beasts
through busy boulevards
And now they don't scare anyone

Too many of our leaders -
are terrified to be honest
As if they were to expose their true face
the greatest sin would be, "to be human"
Power and vulnerability
unbalanced - yet in truth
surrender is the most
immaculate strength

Too many of our lovers -
treat their hearts as slaves
imprisoned in a game of chance
objects in a lottery
Yet in all affairs of the heart
lie pools of limitless creation
no gods or masters
just ever growing ecstasy

Aching for the occult
gushing for more fascination
The weeping astronaut
drifting in abysmal space
Beckoning for ever more discovery
at the cost of his very breath
In every second -
annihilation and ascension
in symbiotic embrace

SHREDDER

The last piece of paper
the last kiss
the last beer
the last chance to pull the trigger
the last night on earth
does it have to mean more?
or anything at all?
Is the story better, if the villan dies?
This is the last piece of paper
the last conversation
I sacrifice it the same way I did the first
with a drink in my hand
nervous blood pooling
in my fingertips
and hope's frail grip
resting on my shoulders

THE TINY PERSON

There is a tiny person
inside the big old man of me
He says things
out of turn
in condescending fashion
with arrogance and
cryptic wisdom

He wants things because
he thinks he knows more than me
He tells me to destroy
everything *I think* I need
because I don't - really
That it will all become worthless
as time unfolds

He tells me to free myself
of all my heavy emotions
to eradicate the phantoms of fear
to buck the fuck up
and take the next load up the mountain
upon a steady back

But he's so small
he's just a little person
And I'm the Big Man!
How could he possibly know anything?
I should just squash the tiny thing inside of me
and be done with it

Alas I cannot -
I'm the bitch and
I'm the little man
He was right all along
This is transient
ephemeral sludge
such brief and fickle things

Nostalgic trash
keeping me from the freedom in my chest
It dims the raging fires in my eyes
I am a hammer - not the nail
I am the rope - not the knot
I am breathing flesh - not the processed meat

The little man grows
and I shrink in turn
We are better than before
and me for having less

THE IIIAD

My life is like an ancient book
stained and torn
bent about and overused

battered and faded
from too many
days sitting in the sun

Strange holes in the paper
with little-to-no memory
as of how they got there

My life is an ancient book
which can now be found
in a thrift store clearance bin

The new vultures
scavenging the pages
oblivious to the myth
that created it

IN BETWEEN

I was on my knees
but I wasn't begging

I was praying
to the only thing
I've ever believed in

The salvation
between her legs

JUMPER

She wears her smile
like the last day on earth

She jumps off every bridge
into a sea of rebirth

All men's hearts collapse
with her little drunken dance

All the world can do is stare
at her sweet hypnotic trance

THE POET WITHOUT A POEM

All these broken minds
and gun-shy egos

All these bruised hearts
and mangled hands

An ever-moving mouth
with nothing to say

These fancy beggars
They don't speak for me

These roadkill tyrants
second hand art dealers

back alley fiends
writhing and bleeding

whining
confused dogs

squealing
confused cogs

These cold fires
They don't represent me

Is all this decay
just a necessary byproduct of our enlightenment?

Must we always pacify each-other like children
With platitudes and straw confidence

Are we always to be held?
to the lowest common denominator?

I summon from the page!
a ruthless warrior of prose

to combat the mob
of mumbling fools

I call forth from this page
with the zeal of a madman

a true sermon of literature
the prowess of death's charm

A sacrifice to the floods of dissolution
An offering to the immaculate tongues

A poet-hero to battle the empty gibberish
of a generation made meek

I shall pull out my very own heart

for the chance
to prove them wrong

THE TECHNOMANCER

Do you ever pray
to electric gods
to blackout the screens?

Get down on both knees
and beg them for silence?
- more precious than any gold

It's like every neuron is occupied
and all every neon light blinks
"No Vacancy"

So full of nothing
So empty of meaning
we forgot to be ourselves

So busy gorging on the news feeds
Saturated in data streams
our lives just passed us by

Do you ever ask the satellites in the sky
to just keep going
to please pass us by?

to halt the transmissions
to let our brains re-align
to the signal of our hearts?

We are insane with information
Sick from lack of substance
corrupted DNA limping along

Our skulls are just cubicles for dollar signs
a trash-bin of files fighting
for space to not be deleted

I'm calling out
for the *technomancer*
in the cloud

to shut it down
for one night
or maybe just a moment

just long enough
for the ghosts to return
to our machines

FREEDOM / MADNESS

A thousand menacing beasts
guard the gates
of lives we long to live

Our hearts held captive -
imprisoned
by an invisible jailor

Feet like ancient roots
cemented to
illusory ground

movements forgotten
we are humbled
by complacency

Despite this
a path unfolds
the night always comes

The clock hands
become our hands
counting moments

The curse is also
the blessing
undisguised

And with this
All fear is slain
All hearts set free

SATURN'S RECORD

I can feel that glorious beat
coming back around again
It's thumping & pulsing
climbing right up to the surface
from the depths of my chest

That spiraling inspiration
coalescing inside my skull
Swarming like supernova hornets
to a swelling hive
stinging me incessantly
with ancient rhythms and perfect pitch

The earth rises up beneath my feet
arching roots creating curious doorways
My body becomes a strobing beacon
A cosmic lighthouse pours from my mouth
All my fingers growing out
like a nervous system of galaxies

I'm so high on organic communication
The doors of perception blasted
right off their hinges
And she is out there somewhere
playing the rings of Saturn
like an old dusty record
and now we dance new life
into this stubborn rock

DEEP SURVIVAL

The mind struts through the halls
of imagination and terror

Fearless of the poet's shadow
- dancing behind the curtain

We lift the words from a blackened mass
and make them walk upon the page

Arcane symbols appear from genetic code
- transcribed upon flesh and paper

The proof of consciousness
slithers between white lines

The progress of a species
dissolves into relentless hunger

We scream out to become more real
than reality can allows

To hell with their death machine!
We will carve a new myth into their heads

There's something profound way out here
beyond procreation and past the Earth's prison

We have discovered Deep Survival!
The voyage of epiphanies - The dive for desolations

We have redesigned our instincts
into exotic desires

We have synchronized all our memories
to fold space and time

Inside the skull of every child
is the hands of Colossus

We are harvesting this cosmic junkyard
for the molecules of our redemption

We are architects limitless and unbound
- reborn in every instant

We are but simple humans
wearing the skin of infinity

METAMORPHOSIS

Her love is a single thread
braided back through the years
that have wrapped me so tightly
into a cocoon of patient change

I await my death
or my transformation
it matters not which one
comes to pass

DEBAUCHERY'S ELITE

We are alchemists
changing maybes into memories

Could-of-should-have-beens
into scrapped elbows and scarred knees

We take the jump
and accept every fall

We take the candy
from every stranger we meet

and no matter how strange it gets
We are the masters of Debauchery Elite!

We are the chemists
taking ordinary

and transforming it
into extraordinary

We are the necromancers
giving everything lifeless

a heartbeat
and new skin

We stimulate pleasure
until it fails

We feel it all until
we go completely numb

BEFORE YOU GOOGLE IT

I don't want to "google it"
I want to talk about it!

I don't want to "just know it"
I want to arrive at the conclusion

I want to meet the girl
and sniff around

Allow her to check out the goods
and let the pheromones to do the talking

I want to discover things
organically

Not thorough background checks
for digital compatibility

How is that natural?
Where is the risk or the value in that?

If you have invested Nothing
then you'll walk away...from everything

I don't want to "google it" – OK?!
I want to sit back in awe
and not know the answer

I want to just sit there and think
about the question

Preserve the wonder
Protect the curiosity

I don't want to become
just another strung out
robot search engine

I don't want to "google it"
I just want to just keep talking - endlessly

under billions of stars
I'll never know the names of

I want to hear you discuss things
fumbling and weaving around "the point"

I want to just listen to the music
before I know who the artist is

I just want to enjoy it
dare I say - just for the fuck of it

No reason
No reason at all

adore the moments
floating in social blackness

enjoying not knowing
before they know it all

FROM NOTHING COMES EVERYTHING

She grips the crescent moon
in her hands
like an eager scythe
All the world stares
as she cuts the sky in two

Every star bleeding
into hollow eyes
Our hearts now tailored suits
cocooning the night
like a wild creature fast asleep

CONFESSIONAL

I was just an old worn-out canvas
hanging in some church of sadness

until she broke in like a bad nun
just to splash me with new paint

with the sealing of her crimson kiss -
is a Renaissance of mystic bliss

NO ZEROS TO CARRY

I don't think you understand
and to be fair
it's highly probable
that the probabilities
are close to or near
impossible -
that you even could
against these odds

Add in the fact
that we are consciously
aware of fractal components
that we cannot in good conscience
subtract from this equation

Subconsciously we plot
the next move without carrying
the zeros back to ourselves
A null set and not one real solution
not to mention
we split the difference even further
between the self and the ego
when we are calculated paradoxes
as if we had the powers
to be something infinitely more
that what we started with
at the vertex of our
graphic origins

Are you still keeping count?
with the rhythms
of our primal nature
clicking like a metronome?

Can you see the pattern?
that our pulsing hearts
make against the map of the stars?

Say a prayer tonight
for all our dead mathematicians
Solve a problem right now
to impress the quantum-magicians
At time collapses
into more and more
nothingness
that's when you know
you've really got
somethingness

for in the center of this spiritual mass
is a scientific petition
to seal magic forever
into divine machinery

THE VANDAL

Praise be
to the
fearless vandal!

Hail to his fire -
made of
new ideas

Hallelujah -
Raise your
glass!

Revel in the remains
of this museum -
the faces in ashes

TYPE-O

There are
no typos
only
ink
that
hasn't
made it
home
yet

THE SPHINX'S RIDDLE

We are
neither ugly
nor beautiful

for' we wear
a thousand masks
yet we have no face

We are not
the pulverized
sand of mankind

but we can feel
their bodies
pass through us

We are truly a mystery
for we could never
understand the answer

WEAPON OF LUST

I wouldn't come up for air now
if she begged me to

I'm too deep inside her grail
to even care where I began

I have discovered some new nectar -
sweeter than all the world's sugar

The honey bees flee the hive
in search of this saccharine paradise

Her moan is a siren
curling my eager bones

I become the weapon of her lust
bursting waves of fluid and flesh

This is the strangest form of hunger
only increasing in need - the more that that you feed

JUST DUST IN A VACUUM

All the once barbarous tanks -
are now covered in wildflowers

Vast seas of blood have dried
and the soil is rich in turn

Bang! Bang! goes the heart's cannon
but only a tiny white flag appears

The vultures pass right by
for there is nothing left to scavenge

Death can no longer be feared
for it has fallen desperately in love

Verdant trees burst
from the world's empty chest

A million microscopic seeds
choke out archaic sorrows

Roots swell and budge
writhing in every tiny follicle

Unseen universes
form and disappear

all within a single moment
bubbling off a grinning skull

The power of many oceans
rises into a single point

yet it flows through us all
just as easily as dust in space

BABBLE BABBLE BABYLON AND ON

This is soft tyranny
This is a strange poison

in a war of broken words
where no one speaks at all

I am the flotsam of a once great ship
drifting in a vast amnesiac mind

I am a criminal upon the gallows
before me a throng of babbling baboons

My head is already within the noose
all I have left is this poetry you see?

I just want to smoke my proverbial last cigarette
and say a few words

but these damned monkeys -
they just want a show!

They scream in my ear,
that "Shakespeare was a myth"
and "all of history is just a twisted lie"

I beg them to just calm down
I try to calm them with a Bard's tale

A story of a trillion perfectly ripe mangos -
an endless and juicy paradise

I tell them I'll weave a glorious climax
about beautiful monkey playmates
with beautiful stunning red asses

I promise to carve out the loveliest of passages
from the halls of their doom and gloom

But these monkeys couldn't care less
they only want to see me suffer

So I lean back upon my nylon hanger
and I send out this little S.O.S

across a digital madness
and a sea of wild simians

A desperate message
at the bottom of a bottle
Hemingway! - please make it quick

A winged prayer
from my drunken lips
Baudelaire! - do you remember the last verse?

I hope in these final moments
swinging in the breeze that
good Ol' Bukowski - can still make me laugh
II

MOONING THE MOON

The moon stares
through the open window
and smiles down a wonderful glow
upon her big beautiful bare ass
A glorious arching curvature
seemingly created in this exact instant
to accommodate the radiance

As I leave this stunning scene
in the early hours of the morning
I look up into the night sky
and wink at the full moon
just before I close the blinds
and head to work with a hard-on

I'LL TRY ANYTHING ONCE -
THEN FORGET I DID IT

Eyes veiled in new memories -
hands lightly dipped in a fragile innocence

dusty cabinets creak open -
revealing mummified documents

orphans caught in limbo -
between a garbage heap and a picture frame

neurons firing like machine guns
at the St. Valentine's day massacre

abandoned composers -
still holding the tyranny of truth

these past lives are like tiny monsters
hiding under the proverbial bed

embedded in the mundane
are all the deepest revelations

creeping around the silhouettes
cast by our amnesia

are hibernating memories
awakening with the fiercest hunger

DRAINED

I keep her in my heart
like wilted flowers
on the windowsill

all the life
drained

all the color
faded

Yet in a strange way
just as gorgeous as
the day I put them there

LIONESS

Her pride
is
covered in
blood -
completely full
of
itself

CONSTANT MIGRATION

I've lost plenty of feathers along the way
but I've never lost my course
Due North motherfucker

you can take your shots at me
you can change the wind's direction
you can put a mountain in my path

you can even poison
all my ink wells

But you better believe -
I'll still be flying home this season

LONG BET

I'm the kind of guy
who will always take the long bet
just to watch her smile

Tonight we break the maiden
Tonight we break her in right

The horses are born wild
It's the saddle and the years
that even out their heads

Tonight we break the bank
We break it wide open

Dollars disappear
as easy as the minutes

We're not in it to win it
we just want to play
for as long as we possibly can

PRISTINE

We would much rather
consume the poison
than be chained to your famine

Our hearts are variegated
striped and stained
with the blood of
all dead poets

Our souls are ancient
they don't bother to die
because they never run out
of trifle things to live for

We hunt the words
that give spiritual
sustenance -
bleed elusive colors

We gather up the pain
and devour it whole
It becomes our energy
beating in tune with the stars

We drink of the darkest waters
and drown in their depths
We emerge cleansed of guilt
strong and pristine

GOLDEN CHAOS

A heart like a wretch
lurking around paradise like a fiend

tonguing the scraps
from their trash cans

feeding open wounds
with the salt of the earth

His heart is mangled
self-inflicted misery

expedite the passions
rush in the ruin

His heart is homeless
torn from the angel's dress

thriving off the eclipsing light
of the passing lovesick fools

His heart is golden chaos
absorbing darkness

and reflecting the brilliant
beauty of isolation

HEADDRESS

I've become a wretched beggar
crawling on the floor
crawling on all fours
crawling for just a bit more

Scouring the former glory
searching in stinking mud
for a once mighty crown
lost in the poetic residue

The only way back
to that holy throne -
a headdress made of gold flesh
and two quivering legs

P O O L I N G

I am a painter
with a palate of pooling red
and no room for faces

I am a sculptor
but I carve with a battle-axe
into precious stones

All my lovers drip
from my fingertips
like the blood off knifes

I've lost track -
but who really wants
to count that high?

I've lost my way -
but there was never
an exit here

I've lost sight -
of the man I was
supposed to be following

DEEP BOTH WAYS

The highs from her affection
sail me so effortlessly over
all of this world's apathies

The lows from her infection
drag me so harshly through
all of this world's tragedies

FIRE DANCE WITH ME

I continue
to pretend
that I am immune
that nobody can hurt me
but the brutal truth is -
that with every word
with every long night
in between the sheets
and every white line
is the perfect potential
to destroy me in full
yet I continue to sit
like a complacent
can of gasoline
surrounded by those
beautiful
dancing
flames

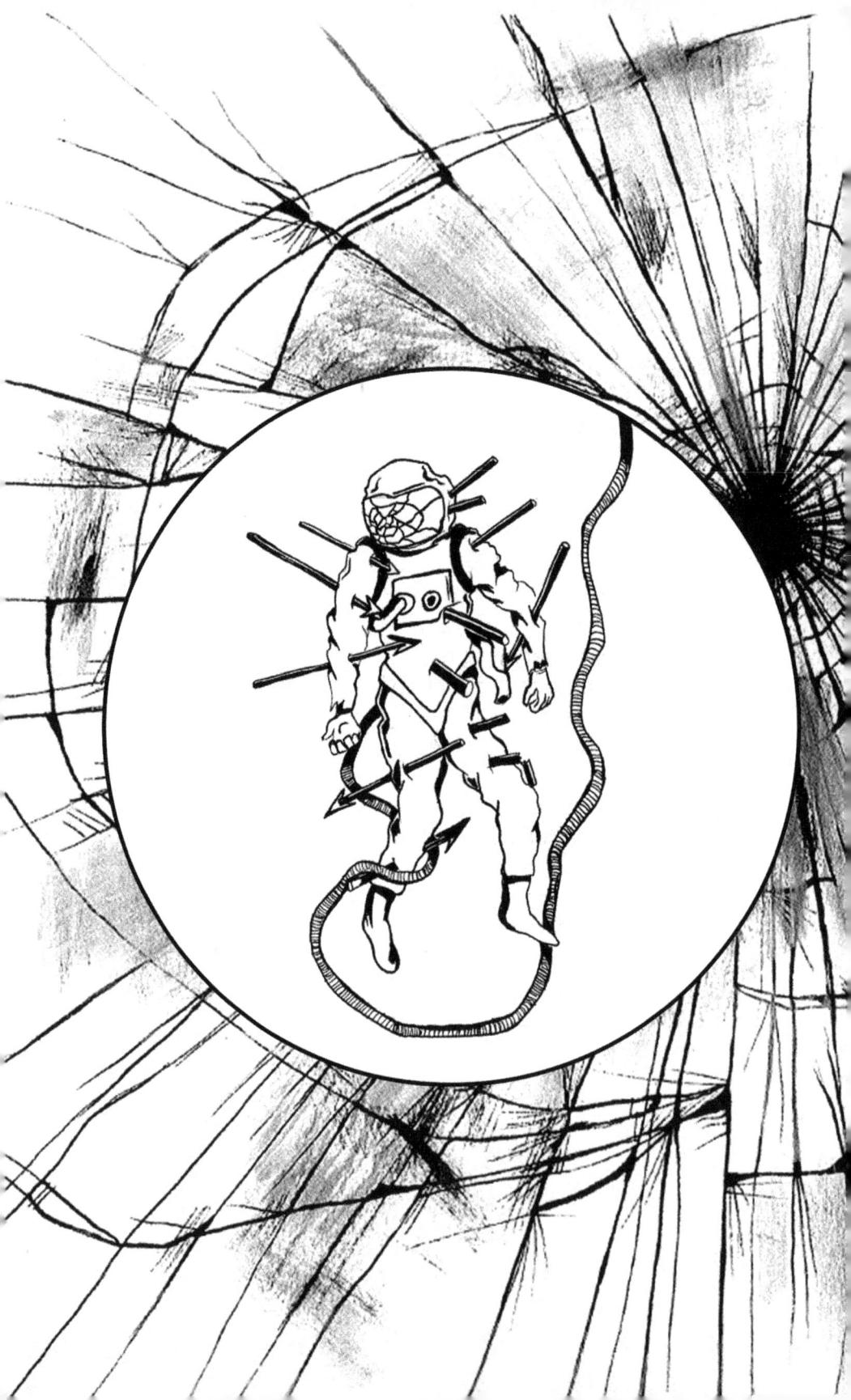

CALIBRATING THE SCALE

Inverted spaces
reveal hidden treasures -
blooming explosions
and sudden surrender

Intricate worlds
folding endlessly -
bloated intellects
crumbling into finite dust

A universe that weighs
nothing at all

Tiny truth
lost in the expanse –
growing courage
laced with shards of doubt

Pulled triggers
release bullet prayers –
sleeping angels
and bloody miracles

Love is measured
in beats per lifetime

Cracked reality
in an ever-changing mirror –
shattered illusions
worshiping reflections

Cosmic fractals
holding precious time -
pushing out
and pulling in

Death is bliss
when you know everything

OUR BLOOD IS THE UNIVERSE'S INK

I wait
for the words to enter me

like a monk sits upon
the cold temple floor

waiting for enlightenment -
And just like that solitary man

poised motionless in mundanity
He expects nothing

He tries
not to try at all

He is the collected sum
He is a billion billion parts

He is life
He is extinction

He is engulfed in flames
sitting as a stone

These poems like packets
of spiritual intelligence

They are all at once
vacuous yet complete

Messages from the
outer-spaces of the mind

Transmissions from the depths
of all our abysmal souls

Both wave and particle
Both here and nowhere
Both the illness and a cure

I am but a brief conduit
for the prose of an infinite cosmos

YET TO BE DISCOVERED

In absentia of myself
detached from anchors of reality

stripped from the core
I float free

fragmented bones
disassociated flesh

Each neuron is a floating island
in a vast electric sea

the symphony of thoughts
conducted with instruments of light

The slowest explosion
is the sweetest death

maximum experience
in the tiniest of moments

I have captured a trillion heartbeats
of a creature yet to be discovered

THE POEM AT THE END OF THIS BOOK!

It's the one you've been waiting for
The big one!
The one to blow your mind apart
The one that changes everything
The one that makes you a believer
The one you can take home to Mom
This is the one - I'm telling you
The one they will talk about for generations
repeat in basement think tanks
Cut up and analyzed by the future elites
Wars will wage in spirit of its prose
This is the one
This is where all the others were leading to
The pinnacle
The zenith of heart and intent
Culminating crescendo of poetic explosion
This is it - right here
This is what it's all about
cause just like the monster
at the end of the book
and much like the light
at the moment of enlightenment
much like the craving
we perpetually quench
This is the one
that we need the most
Ache!
for
the next breath
Seek it
like life
after death

This
is.....
it

ESCAPE VELOCITY

The edge
of the
known universe
is where
my heart
touches hers

We go
as far as
we can

then we go
just a bit
further

WAR PAINT

All this poetry is just
so much war paint
on the face of a tired warrior
Just a few pretty songs
before eventual surrender

DRUNK - THAT'S THE ANSWER

The days I find myself
the most drunk - I swear
are the days I said to myself,
"I'm not going to drink today"
Strange how this iceberg logic
manifests itself
How even when, we only have
one measly person to worry about
in this world
we still fuck it up
9 times out of 10
You can look back
at any human life - I'm betting
and say,
"Wow, didn't see that coming"
So much is a mystery
so much is dumb luck
so much a muddy pool of chance
and only a few pristine pockets
that so few of us
are ever allowed to swim in
So maybe next time
I will try and hack the system
and proclaim,
"I'm getting as drunk as I possibly can today!"
But I think we both know what
will happens then...

LOVE'S ALCHEMY

All pain
is not created equal

It is but the raw material
for our hearts laboratory

We have exactly
one lifetime

to preform
love's alchemy

BETWEEN

We can't
undo
what we've
already done
but we can
do away
with what
we thought
we were

I'll be ready
just as soon
as you
return

Resurrection?
well ...
It's just a state
of mind baby

And last night
we both died
in each-other's arms
between
each-other's legs
over and over
inside each-other's
minds

We rise
from the ashes
of our mistakes
and lick
each-other's wounds
clean of
our
mutual destruction

DAMSEL

Homeless rage
wanders the streets
like a wanted man

A mind salivates
in abundant thirst
for an illusionary bliss

We have a million answers
to questions no one will
ever think to ask

This anger is a vagabond
with a warrant
upon his head

Our hearts are racing wild
like speeding engines
with cut breaks

Our love is tied to the tracks
out there in the darkness
and right before our eyes

Destined to collide
we can't help
but get high off the panic

FOREVER NIGHT

She hides
herself in
the center of the maze

made from
all the hearts
that she has broke

She's lost inside
always starving
for one more

She waits
for the next
to silence her grief

dying stars gaze
upon her dark might
shedding every photon

casting down
that final light
trapped in her eyes

the power
of
forever night

EYES NARROWLY OPEN

Ripped wide awake
and It's all so incredibly real
painfully surreal
I am wet with the stuff of life
screaming, calling out
My blood rushing in my veins
like a frenzied army ready to die
it's all so seemingly impossible - yet here we are
tightly packed into every crevice of the earth
Every conceivable design executed
our imaginations are just playing catch-up
to the insomniac engines of evolution
There are no vacancies here - without destruction
yet we all breath together in some symbiotic bedlam
Setting such trivial limitations for our species
when a kaleidoscope of options
dances endless before our eyes
Manacled willingly to a single cold cell
when the warmth of a trillion suns
awaits our eager virginal flesh
Tethered to the gate like some poor dog
when a feast of glorious proportions
beckons beyond the walls
We need no proof - we need no gods
All we are - we must become

KNOWLEDGE AT ALL COST

We are
lost
in some
modern
Eden

Hiking
through
euphoria -
bleeding
indigo
memories

The nectar of
infinite
apples
drips from our
wild grins

Insanity
is bliss
when you are
drunk
and
god is dead

LOVE'S SIMPLICITY

The most complex
thing in the
universe
is made from
the simplest
of parts

Every word
in the world
can be reduced
to letters
and a few sounds

All fires
starts
with a
spark and
all within
a moment

The Earth's
raging oceans
are but a collection
of tiny
water drops all
"holding hands"

I am reminded
of these things
as I feel
my heart grow
to unimaginable
proportions

NEW MEMORIES AT ALL COST

Will you pull the trigger
if we beg?
Will you let the guillotine
have its way?
We need you to be certain now
We must have your severity

This war is unlike any other
This war is fought invisibly
with neurons and intoxication
We need your heart to transform
into a wild brute
a solider of new memories
These moments
must be gathered by force
It's not about winning
nor to capture hope
This is destruction
of a crippling past
This is a wildfire
set ablaze to make room
for new growth

Will you deaden us with
your violent love?
This war is not a waste
as long as everything dies

MOSH

Her love
is a mosh-pit
and I can't
stop dancing

NULL SET

I have
given
completely up -
on
defeatists

NEW CREATURE

When you've witnessed the wounds
crawl back together
in variegations
in manifold forms
with dire desires -
you learn to anticipate the cuts
yet appreciate the injuries

When you have harbored maladies
beyond grotesque
out past the abyss
heaven's gate locked
decapitations heal like paper-cuts
death is just another round.....
in a children's game

When the pushers get scared to push
and the fear is crippled
When zero is no longer
the lowest number
When your hunger
becomes the hunter
You will howl
like some new creature

S O A K E D

The human race
is speeding toward
some seductive
finish line
But I think I will
take my time with her
and give her lots
of orgasms

The human animal
is rabid with insane logic
some faulty program
unable to shut down
But I think I will
bite the hand that feeds us
and dine like a wild dog
with no master

The human machine
is breaking down
squealing as it dies
such an ugly thing
I think I will
destroy the blueprints
by washing them
in the blood
of a life worth living

ODE TO NINA SIMONE

Last night I kicked on Spotify
made myself a drink
and decided I was going to listen to some Jazz
No more "whomp whomp whomp" of the techno relentless
or the cry-baby "slit-wrist" emotional stuff
that I grew up on
Nor the brutal mathematical metal
that threatens an aneurism
No - tonight is Jazz night
Tonight I'm chilling the fuck out
entering the land of free spirits
because it's all been too much, you know?
the constant stream of vacant information
endlessly feeding - fat with filth
They want to stuff us so full of shit
it will ooze out our pores
No more of that - tonight is Jazz night
slow and methodical
easy and loose
we take our time with the pain
glimpsing every note
because you never know -
the next one may fade
as soon as it leave our lips
These perilous moments
these dire times
they call for the one and only
Ms. Nina Simone
WoW! what a force
so good it hurts
but the misery is placed
just where it belongs
A priestess of soundscape
a sage of emotions
squeezing the emptiness
for a few drops of purpose
I don't resist
I can't argue

I just shut my damn mouth -
and listen
the heart can do the talking
From my heart to Simone
conversing about where we went wrong
And in every note
she forgives us

PURIFIED

I smirk
and laugh
with
the children
of the
damned

as we
skip through
the
purified
nightmare

NEWBORN

There is
a
genesis
in her
eyes
like a new star
and I am
constantly
reborn

QUIESCENCE

I am staring
strait ahead
looking at
nothing important
thinking about
nothing relevant
I am waiting
for no one
not for a god damn thing
sober and still
but high off the possibility
that I could
stay this way forever
I pray to death
that my life
doesn't last

HUMAN

Nobody is lying
if the truth
of being human
has always been
impossible

SORROW IS A SEASON

I sow
these
crooked fields
of pain

with hungry
hands
and
humble heart

so that one day
I may reap the fruit
from the ancient tree
of wisdom

RETIRED

My bones are worn out
and my body is beaten down

but on a moment's notice
I can be ready to scrap for the prize

You can look me in the eyes
and see every battle I've fought

I may not stand up too tall (anymore)
and I don't bother puffing out my chest

I save my energy for my next meal
I'm like the retired greyhound you see

who's just looking for a home
but adopt with caution because

you can take the dog from the track
but can never take the race out of the dog

SOLITAIRE

am a solitary man
but contained in my fingertips
is a horde of eager children

I'm the loneliest of men
but the cults of the literary dead
will never leave me alone

I am a billion scattered words
waiting to be arranged
into sentences only you could love

SWALLOW THE CHILDREN

I am the sculptor...
I gaze upon invisible lines
guiding my hands
to a shifting Valhalla

I visualize the removal
of every part
no longer needed

In the mind's eye -
the masterpiece blooms
and comes to fruition

but unlike this man
I am no perfectionist
I seek no eternal form

For' I am also the butcher!..
and what I must do
must be known

Everything cut away
must provide nutrition
blood for rock

and just as they are
removed
they are consumed

In the end -
there is nothing
left to carve

I have swallowed all my stones
I have swallowed all my stones

SEXTRATERRESTRIAL

She makes the same old positions
seem like alien sex

She resurrects parts of me
I thought impossibly lost

She puts the meat
on these old bones!

She keeps my days moist with life
and my nights even wetter

She blows my mind
She blows my load

Over all she just blows me
completely...away

RUN ON SENTENCE

First there were the ancients
with their incredible awe and fierce curiosity
They traced out the borders
and gave the art a genesis

Then there was Shakespeare
with his strong wet brain
exercising the limits of our psyche
Every high matched - with an incredible low

Followed by democratic idealists
designing utopias in their heads
building impossible perfections
waiting like gods in psychic palaces

Then came the beatdown
and boy did they beat beat beat us down
into pulpy fictional versions of ourselves
freedom will never look the same

Then comes the righteous babies
with no use for pens
USB ports in their skulls
rearranging letters to form simple abominations

What will the next wave bring?
Cheers! Here's to never shutting up

UNTITLED

Sometimes
the most powerful
of our connections
is contained in
a gossamer touch

SHORTCUT

We dance slow
yet our hearts beat
such furious sounds

We are captured
yet far from
imprisoned

There is a strange
and crooked road
in both of our minds

It is a shortcut
through -
the forest of our pain

ODE TO A RITUAL

I plan on typing
till these fingers are callused
and they can no longer feel the keys

I intend to type
until my eyes are bleeding
and they can barely make out the words

I plan on writing
till I no longer understand -
why the hell I began

I'm writing at gun point
I'm writing in a free fall
I'm writing in the center of the flame
the phoenix that does not return

This room is slowly filling up
with stacks of maybes
and piles of paper-hope
in every shade of desperation

This floor is a sea of abortions
just layers of the dead
a graveyard of unknown soldiers
ink sealed in parchment tombs

My desk is an alter
A testament to my resolve
stained and imprinted
a throne of scars

Mauled by all the lonely nights
it has a patina etched by regurgitated thoughts
thrown back into a cruel world

My typewriter is a sacrificial pedestal
A shrine to strangers
that wait like vernacular fiends

This machine is a slow pistol
firing syllables like bullets
loaded in the barrel of my mind

landing in the retinas of your eyes
pushing and swimming into wet brains
drowning hopelessly in a thick neuron soup

I plan on typing
giving birth to endless creatures
even though I know they are all doomed
fated to be forgotten

UNTITLED

swallow
the
universe

shit
yourself
out

WET GRAFFITI

She is the wet graffiti
in my run-down art gallery
She colors way outside
all my jagged lines
No single frame
could ever hope to contain
the beauty of her heArt

ARTISTIC TRIGLYPH

the written word -
Imprinted incantations
for bringing reality to
its knees
Possession of the mind
to engage powers far beyond
its own comprehension
Psychological magic
bending and folding
all experience into a
pinpoint

sexual transcendence -
Flesh as the medium for new creation
moaning symphonies of madness
orgasms rushing up like the high notes
of a cosmic score
composers hands
dancing in the shadow of divinity
fevered waves of pleasure
pulling infinity within its grasp

mindful intoxication -
The most important of our craft
humbling trances and meditated destructions
precision instruments
carving beauty into the fabric of the unknown
an endless trip of the imagination
the frenzied genesis
liberated love

ACHERONTIA STYX

Study the madness
from within
to become sane

Stand upon
the very edge
to truly understand

Bleed out
and be born
once again

Give everything
to taste
the last drop

Look death
strait in
her eyes

For her love
just might
save us tonight

UNINTENDED

Just remember –
the death
of the
spider
is the
bloom
of the
flies

THE ART OF

once again
they lied to us

It's not beauty
It's chemistry

It's not just love
It's compatibility

It's not intelligence
It's wisdom

It was never strength
It's resolve

It's not power
It's survival

And most
importantly of all

It wasn't self-actualization
It was just maintenance all along

THE SKY IS AN ENDLESS OCEAN

There is a vast and crazed
desire that dwells within me
to control it all
to consume everything
to put my mitts around the world
long enough to shove down my throat
I wish to swallow it down
and allow it to transform me
by destroying me
Like an impossible drug
that induces an infinite trip
Becoming an organism
far beyond the capabilities
of our current biology
Some divine sci-fi self-apocalypse
A sacred death march
to return to a singular
molecular source

There is a simple and humble
desire that hides inside me
to just disappear
to fade quietly away
to just sneak into the darkness
silently so no one will notice
I wish to be unborn
and to have never been at all
by un-creating me
Like a life in reverse
rewinding before the start
A creature unbecoming
clean and pristine
pure in all the glory of nothing
Some holy fantasy self-reconstruction
A sacred death march
to return to a singular
molecular source

YET TO BE DISCOVERED

Your art
has displaced my routine
of taking this wealth of pleasure
for granted
The nets of my vision
now tied to you

Your art
has peeled away
the sheath of fear
revealing
the bright blade beneath

Your art
has removed
all the decaying flesh
allowing seeds by the thousands
to sprout from my every confine

Your art
gives me sensual blasts
without moving at all

Your art
pries open the flower -
too scared to bloom

Your art
galvanizes
endless victory

Your art
Is the caress on the head
of dying men

Your art
is the green grass
at the nuclear test site

Your art
Is a cure
for undiscovered heartache

TRANSMUTATIONS

Horde the hate
of your enemies
like precious fuel

Incinerate it
in the furnace
of your heart

Sit back and witness
the alchemy
of love

PUREST FORM

You can be sure of one thing in this life
The barbarians are coming...
They will arrive
in full mob fashion
with clubs raised
and brains brimming
with a terrible confidence

They will level your logic
Lay waste to your peace
Urinate on all that you hold dear
They shall make a mockery
of your precious art
Deface the most beautiful
of your galleries

The barbarians are indifferent
they are maniacs of senseless power
They feel nothing that is tangible
no compassion to plead to
no prize they acknowledge
I offer no advice
no solution
no absolution

For the barbarians are many
They are ubiquitous
The barbarians are coming
and our triumph
shall come from the fire
We must set our own work ablaze
incinerated by the creator's hands

A Faustian bargain
The consciously destroyed mandala
Free from adulteration
Kept from their radical mutations
Death in its purest form

THE REASON

I write to tell a story
albeit a strange one
to expose a beast's true nature
to release the pressure
of an unbearable heart
to vindicate all my most beautiful sins

I write to tell the stories
of all those soldiers
that died on wild nights
of entire wars
fought between sheets
of a world tilled over
the edges of every moment

I'm writing now
because all your words
just weren't enough
they left me hollowed
and wanting so much more
they reeked of desperation
straw-men holding on to burning prayers

I write because I must
because these fingers are atomic
glowing with such abundance
exploding with uncontainable energy
weird light that cannot be hidden

I write these words to breath into ancient lungs
to blow the dust off our favorite records
and hear music's virginity once again
to exhume our true hearts
from the grave they have become

THE FRACTAL

I draw a shape upon my chest
It's no particular shape at all
But it looks sort of pretty
sort of powerful and strange
A little esoteric and with a bit of the occult
I like the shape
I think I'll carve it into my skin
I think I'll let it stay awhile
I will give it my energy
and I will feed it my spit and my spirt

The shape has begun to mutate
I think it's evolving
the shape becomes so much more
than before
The scattered lines
have spawned
ever more intricate line forms
Now the shape
is a thing all on its own

The shape discovers its name
"Desire"
The shape lives
and the shape grows
I couldn't erase it now if I tried
I don't think it would care if I cried
begged or prayed for it to leave
The shape is no longer mine
It is no longer confined to my chest
It's bigger than my comprehension

I am now but a facet
inside its intricate design
I am just a speck
watching it infinitely bend

YOU ONLY HAVE TO BE GREAT ONCE

All the greats that came before
they're standing tall
and ominous
lurking over my shoulders
casting impenetrable
shadows upon the paper

Bukowski always had the best laugh
but he's laughing at Me now
he's drunk off his ass
and burping in my ear
telling me
"just keep hammering the keys and bleed kid, the
writing part is easy"

Baudelaire is doubled over
crumbled in a strange pile in the corner
choking down some strange elixir
gloom surrounds him as he looks up at me
with those deep sullen eyes and whispers
"you're not drunk enough to be great"

I'm writhing in my seat just to stay alert
combating myself to not throw in the towel again

Plath can be heard from the other room
typing furiously
each letter she executes
transforms into a swarm
of bees threatening me with a
sudden death

I'm dragging my fingers
across the keys like they were in WWI trenches
I'm casting each word
like a grenade into the open world
just hoping they land on the enemy
and not all my friends

Baker and Williams just left
to get more booze and TP
They probably won't be back
anytime soon
not until they've started
some revolution

Rimbaud isn't present
but he left me with the impression
that this poem is like a season
and it's coming to a close
so I better do something prodigious
and do it soon

Have I said everything I can say?
Or am I spent like a six-chambered revolver
Exhausted like a light bulb
left on for the holidays

I can hear Hemingway out back
firing off the shotgun and bellowing
to Thompson that I must, "Cut out the fat! "
I just can't seem to figure out
exactly what that means

I'm crawling across the battlefield now
I'm completely lost as to where I might be going
I feel wounded and terrified
but I'm as safe as a baby
writing behind these comfortable bedroom walls

Ginsberg and Kerouac are arguing on the couch
beating out the details of style and form
one is barking at me to just keep going
drive the thing off a cliff
the other says I should stop and polish what I've got
into a perfect shiny turd

I'm spinning like a top
I feel like I might vomit
Some spiritual pressure is building
within my skull
I feel as if I'm going to Pop!
But I can't abandon this war
I've got to salvage something
resurrect a piece of myself from this tragedy

Everything is invisible
All is as lost as it began
Nothing survives for long
In the end all we had
was a glimpse
of an impossible beauty

THE DIFFERENCE

Love
is what
remains
in the
morning

Lust
is the
stain
on the
sheets

UNWRITTEN

If there's
no story -
than
there's
no hope

ASCENSION

These nights are nectar
creeping up the spine
- slowly ascending

like ancient vines
destined to crawl to the top
- past heaven's canopy

serpentine poison lies
in saccharine fang
- fusing the tail of duality

venom drips
from electric kisses
- love is surrender

the deadliest
are often the most beautiful
- of all things

[MUTATION : SELECTION]

DEEP SURVIVAL

RYAN MORROW

POETRY

RAPTURE OF THE DEEP

SUNKEN TREASURE

Beyond a fresh breath of air
She's a brand-new lung

More than just a quick kiss
She takes all tongue

In the faintest of touch
she calms the most wild of my beasts

In the briefest of moments
is the most filling of all feasts

Withered to a pointed edge
I am cut to her pleasure

Lost deep in love's madness
I drown in her treasure

Buried by pheromonic hands
I am tied to her holy ground

Entranced by sunken eyes
I can never leave - spellbound

THE ODYSSEY BEGINS

I know what I desire
and I will express it
in multitudes
in exquisite detail
in absurd colors
in imaginary fluid exchange
by having sex with the gods

I can no longer wet their broken tongues
I can no longer mend their mangled hands
I can no longer repair their failing machines
I will no longer wait within the quicksand
No one is saved if we both die

I know what I want
and I shall crawl
through all their hells
to have it

SISYPHUS TO THE STONE

Courting you was a wicked dance
Our bodies writhing to crooked beats
Our feet smoldering on hot coals

We would endure the zenith of pain
in exchange for a few bursts of ecstasy

There is truth in
the paradox of love
alongside
a thousand tiny lies

You had the most seductive of kiss
Your saliva was the nectar of bliss
yet our chemistry could only make poison

We drank each-other's Kool-Aid
strait from the vein of pleasure's terminus

Drowning in
crystalline agony
a union of
perfect parasites

Entering you was the unfolding of a deep coil
Our orgasmic howls were crowning signals
to all the dying stars - to know our wreckage

I am bound
to you
as Sisyphus was
to the stone

INSPIRE ME

You inspire me
through bloodshot eyes
through the toughest of times

You inspire me
to bleed
far past the pain

To dig deeper
even when
the ground turns cold

You inspire me
to weather the storms
to smile -
when there is only doom

You turn to me
covered in filth
and your face says it all
"you couldn't stop now, even if you wanted to fucker"

and we laugh without
moving our mouths

we raise our bottle to the new moon
and down what's left of the night

We know this too will pass -
slip into the past

but the poetry-
the poetry will surely last just a bit longer

UNTITL ED

We are
beautifully
crafted
keys
jammed
into
worn-out
locks

INSTINCTS NEVER DIE

With his every breath out
a funeral for powerless gods
and each breath in
a grave-robber who wakes up the dead

The sky is filling up
with invisible destroyers
amassing secret plans
as the earth is swelling with ancient dread

He stalks the days sunlight
like a rabid dog driven by the virus
wild desire in a foaming mouth
the reason has been lost - yet the creature must be fed

<u>A M N E S I A D D I C T</u>

The longer he goes down
into that soft ocean
of tranquility
the less chance he has
at returning the same man

He enters the wild and
the wilderness becomes him
He runs for his life -
runs until he forgets
what he's running for

Under the reflected light
of a forgotten sun
A creature collapses
and crawls into his den
A beast no more

As he falls into
a long hibernation
he gives praise
and asks unnamed deities
that these memories
will fade

REFLECTING BLACK

How dare you stop now.
Just as our fingers come alive.
Upon the zenith of our heart's awakening.
Our minds quivering - so close to release.
How could you pull away now?
Our pain provides no tantric reward.
The prize of our toil beckons.
The art from our gushing wounds.
The taste so sweet it destroys all that came before.
How can you pass by such orgasmic waters?
We craft ourselves a beautiful suit of armor to protect
us from ourselves.
We create such magnificent vessels to sail us further
from each other.
How is it possible not to surrender now?
We have polished the void into a perfect reflection.
It shines so bright - its origin forgotten.
Is the knowledge that you are but a lynchpin
and not the entire machine
- any less exquisite?

BLOOD ON HEAVEN'S GATE

Who needs a crown
when this kingdom is free

Wrapping her legs around my skull
I don't intend to ever surface

Death by dissolving -
the torture of an endless orgasm

Resurrection
is a kiss

How many lifetimes have existed
between these sheets?

If god had a gun and told me to stop
I'd be a bloody mess on heaven's gate

QUEEN OF THE NIGHT

I am just a thorny cactus
drying in the desert sun

But that never stopped her
from blessing me with her kisses

Visiting me in the death of this night
showering me with salvation

A beautiful flower blooming
everywhere she made contact

MY CULT IS BLACKER THAN YOURS

cult, cult, cult
religion
cult, cult, cult
religion
cult, cult, cult...

We keep sifting
through the same
damn sand
looking for
new gold

We dig and dig
in the same
tired hole
expecting to find
new treasures

cult, cult, cult
religion
tribe
pack
group hug
It's all the same tired tune
to the same ol' song
the same worn out mantra
begging like two prostitutes
for both sides to win the game
There is only one prize

And it's given to everyone
no matter what team
you happen to be on

Death is
the ultimate touchdown

BLOOM AND DIE

My arrogance
made it impossible
to love me

My obsession
created terror
behind my eyes

Our lust
destroyed
the innocence
of every virgin night

We incinerated
upon contact
We bloomed and died
in an instant

I wait always
in these embers
for just one more chance
to light up the sky

THE TERRIBLE ITCH

She would let me fuck her
like I loved her
Yet she always refuses
my flowers
She would suck my dick before
and after sex
But she would rarely let me
kiss her in the morning

We had the time of our lives
but her life didn't have the
time for mine
I was wild for her every inch
she only wanted me
when she couldn't scratch
the itch

As she became satisfied
I grew ever more hungry

THEY DON'T WRITE THEMSELVES

I can't avoid her forever
She waits there
patient and
calm
staring straight through me

I know what she wants
I can give it to her
just the way she likes it
I know just what to say

yet still I walk by
still I pace around the throne
strolling right past
 her siren calls

I am the coward
the failed hero
my sword covered in dust
my heart rusted from neglect

She is there waiting
begging for her knight
beautiful and helpless
I know what I must do

yet I stroll by
with my head down
eyes squeezed tight
I just can't avoid her forever

And just when all hope is lost
A bottle is cracked
a drink is poured
and the reason reappears

I know just how this ends
with the fire of
Hephaestus in my gut
I return to war
I sit back in the chair
and begin to write again

EVAPORATED

Fractured images spiral
cluster and swarm

Forming a skull
in the chaos

Each moment another fang
in a mouth growing so wide

Every flavor of madness
floods the palate

While the guts form
impossible knots

The heart sinks further
and further down

Some black anchor that falls
toward an infinite below

Peace is an abstraction
created for divine laughter

Vile fingers ooze in denial
across the vacant alter

The stench of prayer
embedded in the pages

Another S.O.S. thrown
into an crowded glass ocean

long ago made barren
from our relentless apathy

SPILLED INK

The pen is useless
when the ink
has no story

The typewriter
is only an anchor
to the selfish heart

All the literature in the world
cannot save
a wasted life

FLAT CIRCLE

Your skin
pines to become
my skin once more
But time has
stood sentry
against our union

Our memories
are now like silence
caught between
the raindrops
trapping
our intentions

We deny the river's end
We deflect the kiss of the blade
We are freaks of lust
We fuck
but never touch
We speak
but never say a word

Tantric and sadistic
I chase you
and you chase me
but we never
catch a thing

BLACK RAIN

this black rain
won't water anything
a garden grows
crooked - mangled fruit
But a single red rose
blooms in the graveyard
of a once mighty heart
trying to push its beauty
with sylvan strength -
but the world is taciturn
with no one left to impress

IT'S JUST DESSERT

The pain
feels good

when you know
you deserve it

UNLEARN

We've been playing
with fire
like we're made
from the flames
themselves

We choose
to dance
upon the knife's edge -
as if our scars
can't remember
their ache

These days baby
they've kept us too far away
but our hearts -
they want what they want
and god damn if they don't
always get their way

THE UNLOVABLE

Do you feel better?
Knowing what it is she really desires.
Are you more at ease?
Holding the knowledge she once withheld.
Can you bear to face yourself now?
With her light no longer pointed in your direction.
Are you any better off now?
Now that the hammer of truth has smashed the remaining hope.
Can a man be stronger than his heart's desire?
Will you watch as your futures burn before your eyes?
Would the silence be your savior knowing what you know now?
Can she just keep blooming infinitely brighter?
Will she ever find what it is she's not looking for?
Is her kiss the kiss of a better death?
Will the tight rope she walks upon ever pull down the sky?
Can she keep dancing through the flames and never feel a thing?
Does she dream of power? Or to be worshiped? An army at her feet?
Does she know the empire is hers to command?
I lie at the bottom of all this
naked and unarmed
a drowned man
in his own self-inflicted sorrow
Words like anvils
hold me to the seafloor
my voice is as useless
as an underwater bird
She will fuck everyone
just to find something new
I can't fuck anyone
that doesn't remind me of her

S C H I S M

that love
was never one thing

chimera -
shifting bliss

merging bodies
blending minds

heads of lust
tales of romance

She drove me mad
and I became the madman

She made me wild
and I became as wild as can be

love so crazy
it drove off every ledge
I became two men
one that burned with passion

fighting for infinities
raging like divinities
a devoted warrior
in the quicksand of time
And the one that knew better -
a fading masterpiece
a shattered teacup
never to reassemble

the man at odds
against himself

neither man
could possibly prevail

a schism
parasitic duel

One man could only surrender
and the other flee

THE GRAVE OF HESITATION

I hesitate to break the stillness
caught between our hearts

I lurk like a fiend
behind an unbroken veil

My eyes salivate
to see you in full

My hands shedding –
they feel brand new

Every night I burst into flames
kept from your ocean and it's waves

I am the rabid silhouette
that dances in your shadow

A grand mystery trapped
inside the seconds we can't touch

<u>NECROMANCER</u>

Supple hands
caress the dead
and tempt the demons
from their sleep

Dancing
on the
tip of
doom itself

Pleading
with angels
for just
one more

kiss
Calculating
the risk and
licking around
a burning

fuse
Tasting
the danger
in every

moan
Gripped in-between
stone thighs

Clenched in-between
bitter teeth

a rusty key
opens no doors

PRETENDER

Turtles all the way down
Death all the way through

You will find me somewhere
at the bottom of this

I awake
peeling guilt from my eyes

I begin to doubt my own existence
until it pulls me to the commode

I realize I will never die or
I'd be dead already

Walking in circles -
always descending

This Hell is not a place
it is an arrogant denial

This hell is spiritual weight-lifting
until you can hold something hollow

I am fighting of an ambiguous swarm
with disappearing arms

I am not blind
but rather seized

by a pounding strobe of
clarity and desperation

When everything is so free
and completely available

what is it really
that's left to desire?

Is it the yearning itself
that we can't live without?

Is it "the having"
that kills us?

All these corpses
in constant surrender

yet we are at war
with their infinite armies

Let's play a game! - but first
you have to pretend you're dead

FIRE-SALE

In the wake
of
your
self-destruction
is your
greatest
artwork

In the trail
of
your
pain
is the
deepest
wisdom

Within
all
your
heartbreak
is the
truth
of love

<u>ADAPTATION</u>

False kings stand sentry to a kingdom of filth
atop their empty heads - a plastic crown

Calling out demands from a rotting throne
they rummage through the hollow of their minds

grasping with desperation
at some evanescent meaning

Their ego is an anchor
sinking into astral quicksand

the words are tattered ropes
that cannot pull them out

The deceivers must be hung
to extol the true magic

in their swinging silhouettes
is the most poetic of justice

in the bloodbath of chaos
is a golden truth

To give creative birth
is to feel the weight of it - pain

It must pass through
the keyhole of doubt and fear

screaming with viridian eyes
howling with zealous desire

to grow out of control
to be planted in the soil of chance

THE CALL OF THE CERBERUS

There is nothing quite like black lace
strapped tight across porcelain skin
I could die there
or maybe just incubate
buried inside the perfection of that sin
I am no longer a man
just a deranged creature lost in the wild
I cease to be sentient
simplified into pure instincts

Raven hair flowing through me
pouring endless
wraps me in timelessness
a death clock
I will never leave this
if I don't have to

Penetrating far beyond the climatic
these rewards are intergalactic
It's all too much
yet I must have more
Violence is symbiotic with its thirst
The depth of which keeps me curst

The limits of our lust drifting ever further out
wound after wound a body suffering becomes devout
Union of incredible power
two super-massive particles of love and lust
resonating profound
emitting light all around

Love yours truly,
- the Hellhound

<u>HYENAS</u>

They're at it again
the hyenas
cackling
laughing
taunting me
They're crowding my skull
with their secrets
Spit it out beasts
Reveal yourselves!
Cough it up
I can see them
smiling
grinning
through blood soaked snouts
They have so much to feed on
yet their hunt never ends
They drown me in madness
even sleep can't save me
Be gone vile fiends!
this carcass is barren
the bones polished
They're at it again
those hyenas
with every laugh they multiple
compounding my terror
growing my fears
And now I begin to laugh
just like before
I can taste the metallic blood
pooling in my mouth
It makes me laugh all the more
hysterical and wild
I look for the mad creatures
and see nothing around

alone at long last

PLUCKING THE PEARL

Beneath the husk
of these brief lives
is an infinite love

To unearth
the treasure is
to seek its depths

To pluck
the pearl is
to leave a bruise

Shedding pain
like so much skin -
layer by layer

Swimming down
through time's gravity –
hour by hour

we disappear

THE AUTOPSY

On display
on display
everybody on display
like an autopsy

we are splayed out
and they are all
looking in

to see the helpless things
we are within

We are all trapped
inside
looking out
at their scalpel eyes
and surgery grins

There is a mystery here
held tight
and kept in

that's the point

to keep
the
mystery
burning

sew
yourself
shut

UNTITLED

Death
is a whore
and we all
sleep with
her
eventually

ULTRAVIOLET

We kiss in the strange glow of atomic light
while the symphony of denial
pulls apart our angry hearts

We dance like savage pagans
reading poetry in the flames
seeing gods in the ashes

We're in love with the death
of all our moments -
our bliss tied to destruction

The extinction of our fear
is the birth of a creature that cannot be killed
by violence or ultraviolet light

S K I N

She keeps me
nuzzled and tucked -
comfortable in my own skin

she subdues them -
the beasts from crawling
out from within

There is a constant war
just beneath
the soft surface

The soldiers of anxiety
ready to match the world
to the blackness in their eyes

But with her simple touch
they retire in an instant
combustion of flames

With the curl of her lips
an army destroyed
a treaty signed

She keeps me
in a comfortable prison -
a den of beautiful sin

GATEWAY DRUG

falling
in love
is by far
the most
dangerous
drug
you
could
ever consume

I recommend
building
up
a good
tolerance
first

THE INEVITABLE DECAY

There is an eloquent mind here
but it is now imprisoned -
fear surrounds it like starving jackals
feeding on the tiniest morsels

A brilliant sculptor
exiled to an island -
with nothing more
than mud and river stones

The best you can do
is hardly good enough
when the best you were
was better than the rest

HOUSE OF CARDS

She was the queen of my heart sitting on her throne
and I was the jack of spades sitting all alone -
We were one ace away from taking back Rome
Now I am the headless king without a home
only memories and a sinking catacomb

There's a casino in her eyes
for which my heart could not help but rise -
this broken crown I do despise
a poison kingdom full of lies -
now you shall find me where death cries

GORGON PARADOX

He opened up his lungs
in an attempt to breathe in something new
anything *new*

He spread his arms wide
in hopes of catching a passing vibration
any feeling at *all*

Not quite dead
but far from truly alive
a pulse with no beat

Lost at sea
he is carried further out
with each collapsing waves

Drowning in doubt
the very air around him
is a stone man's grip

His future is nothing more
than a crowd of Gorgons
staring right at him

With his eyes held shut
he dare not make a sound
existence in perfect patience

UNDER THE MICROSCOPE

Plucking them one by one
from the mob of societies rotting orchard

They are examined
under the microscope of skepticism

We just had to know
what was on the inside

Can't say we're really that impressed
Can't say we're surprised by what we found

Just a bunch of loose parts
cheap imitations
and broken egos

Dirty love
desensitized optics
and a lot of bloated memories

Nothing much worth saving
or attempting to fixing
mostly what we found
was just a whole lot of bullshit

CONTRA-DICTION

Immaculate introspection
Desperate resurrection

We rise
We rise
from the ashes
of our past lives

survival
is the most
intoxicating
of our drugs

Some days filled
with life's ecstasies
all the others kept
in full shade -
a sun gone missing

Exotic surrender
Eternal splendor

We fall
We fall
Down from such great heights
into dark pools

death
is the most
seductive
of our drugs

When the days burn too bright
and blind our visions
Even beauty is a flood -
sent to drown our hearts

Radical vitality
Extreme duality

We are absolutely
everything
and yet we will never be
anything at all

MIXED SIGNALS

Drugs in the operating room - Needed
Drugs for the death-rattle - Necessary
Drugs for religious theatre - Acceptable
Drugs for the military advantage - OK
Drugs that are "approved" by the FDA - OK
Or by the PhD signature - OK
Drugs that the government can profit from - OK
Free drugs - Always Bad
Drugs for recreational use - Bad
Drugs for mind expansion – Extremely Bad
Drugs for coping - Bad
Drugs that make you curious - Bad
Drugs for increased intimacy - Bad
Drugs that open and heal the mind - Very Bad
Dissociative Drugs - Great
Hallucinogenic Drugs - Unacceptable
Inebriating Drugs - OK
Stimulating Drugs - Bad

I don't know about you -
but I'm getting mixed signals...

U N T I T L E D

this love
may cut you
but it will
also patch
you up

this love
may burn you
but it will
also
cleanse you

My love
will destroy us
but we will
both be
better for it

DOJO NO-MO

I was once
an isolated
peaceful temple

nothing changed
nothing was out of place
nothing needed repair
only a bit of preventive maintenance
It was the
meditation of the dead
But along came
a
pretty
creature

O' so cute
and ever
so cunning

cuddly
with
claws

That creature walked
that creature stalked
and that creature grew

It was
multiplying
madness
Like a sw
elling wave of fire
my walls - they flooded
with those flames

My quiescent dojo
torn asunder

"When the fire reaches the heart
it's best to just sit back
and enjoy the light show"
I said, as my temple burned
to the fucking ground

SIN IS EDUCATION

They sent the hellhounds
to take me down

but those dogs
only cleaned my wounds

They licked me
free of my guilt

They polished
my sins into pride

The hounds and I
are the same breed

We howl in concert
We howl in tune

We howl without fear
We howl to no moon

Together we chew away
the chains of absolution

<u>WHEN SHE RETURNS</u>

When she walks away
from me
the romance
goes as well

When she walks away
my lips crack
with the
vacancy

She is only ever gone
for a short time
but my rooms are so hollow
in the absence

The oceans of poetry
temporarily quelled
The darkening surface
taunts with patient power

Down in the depths of me
is slowly rising
ten-thousand creatures
to taste her once more

HEART LIKE A TOMB

Long ago
a heart was buried
deep in the depths
of burned soil

Since that day
two hands crawl
begging to bloom
from the surface

reaching out
to grasp new doom
better to remain
beneath the earth entombed

LONG AFTER

Beware!
her
severed-head
still
just might -
turn you
to
stone

RACE TO NOWHERE

The human race
needs a fresh coat of paint

Our brains are filthy
and need a long bath

The human race
is overdue for its check-up

Our egos could
benefit from a cold shower

The human race
needs a rewrite

Our mouths
fitted with a muzzle

The human race
needs a clean pair of underwear
Our government needs more IQ points
and our military a bit more compassion

The human race
is still sleeping
late for the next evolution
and needs a god damn wake-up call!

ANCIENT EYES

There is a powerful yet
dangerous woman before me

She is painted in the blood of a heartbroken man
She is dressed in a strange and frightening unknown

New shades of black
Ancient dying eyes

Despite the phenomenon displayed before my eyes
I cannot look away -

for' the creature has a perfect dance
for' the creature is a death trance

She spins and twirls with impossible ease
She ungulates her foreign body to divine rhythms

I am hypnotized
I am paralyzed

I dare not
deny her audience
With each sharp turn
With every glitch of her steps

A buried secret revealed
A revelation emerges

Infinities are born
And as if life itself was trapped beneath her dress

She pirouettes like an insane top
and the universe is revealed

The umbrella of death has opened
to reveal an even more beautiful exit

RORSCHACH IN THE FLAMES

Loving her
was a head on
collision

Although
we both
survived

I was unable
to pull my heart
from the wreckage

EAT YOUR FATE AND LIVE IT TO

Sometimes
you just have to start
from the bottom
in order to understand
the fall

And sometimes
you must devour everything
to know what you had
at all

ETERNAL DAMNATION

Auto-erotic mastication
I am consuming
parts of myself
just to get through to her

Seducing death
to play with my heart
because this sinuous carnage
has never been more attractive

The more you bleed for it
the more you love it
Her eyes are teeth
and my body is raw meat

Our lust is
limitless
and my imagination
never sleeps

She has provided such
a supreme temptation
We are now slave and master
to each-others abyss

Her wicked dance
has become
but spiritual lingerie
over top an open grave

I am possessed
by her danger
This intoxication
is worth eternal damnation

TWO FINGER DISCOUNT

She is
the liquor -
on the
top shelf

but she
never
makes me
reach

CARNIVORE FOR HER

I am the smiling wolf
at the end of his hunt

She is the blood
reflecting in the moonlight

A POEM ABOUT NOTHING

The fear is nothing now
a mere scratch
on the hide of
the grizzly bear

I'm strutting down the
darkest alleys now
I couldn't be stopped
by a thousand of their thugs

Hell!
I can't understand
why we didn't just
do this in the first place

The orchestra is
really turning up now
blowing all the horns
a crescendo for good measure

I got a strong feeling
about how
this one's going
to end

My chest is all puffy
guts made of steel
I'm the boss
tonight's my night

The drinks
going down
like flimsy
tin soldiers

Tonight
I think
I'll be
the story

Some other sap
can
write it
down

WATCH IT ON TV

This city is killing me
slowly draining my confidence
and chopping away at my heart
cutting it into pieces too small
for anyone to see

It's dissolving my mind
washing it with powerful bleach
and tossing all my memories
into the trash

This city is killing us
It's strangling the smile from
our nervous faces
It's holding our heads
just below the horizon

It's making our sex
shameful and mechanical
It's caging up our instincts
wearing away our claws
filing down our fangs

Here we are neutered and tame
Now we watch it on TV

This city is killing itself
wrapping the ancient telephone lines
around our billboard necks
hanging itself
and never knowing why

This city is dead
and we all walk around the asphalt
like a funeral possession
just ghosts haunting
the empty streets

Cold bodies
casting mangled silhouettes
across a neon sky

EVERY NAME IN THE BOOK

sweetheart
asshole
genius
idiot
lover
player
god
animal
genuine
liar
lunatic
humble
loser
stud
boring
too intense
passionate
indifferent
evil
compassionate
renaissance man
drunkard
sexy
disgusting
brilliant
hack
weirdo

I've been called every name in the book
I'm all of them and somehow none of them
I blame genetics

THE DEFINITION

Ability to dance like children gone mad
Summon the music from the floorboards
Fearless to push the levers to maximum capacity
See an ocean separate from the power of our tongues
To raise a glass and drink with the demons in our heads
To coil a single night into the palms of our hands
and make it seem like it just might be –
the entire universe

INVERSE SQUARED

I must
have been
in love
with
you not
loving me

AT NIGHT

The prettiest
of her flowers
always bloom
when their asleep

The brightest
of her petals
drowning
in a sea of darkness

UNCONDITIONAL

She pulls the trigger
the bullet rips through my chest

I don't panic
I don't break

All I can do is admire
that shooting stance and her slender hips

She pours the fuel
doubling an already burning fire

It's not the flames that burn me
It's that crooked smile on her lips

A witch's smirk can be so cruel
as her ritual takes ever higher

She grips a wicked blade
casually sinking it into my gut

I don't scream
I don't throw a fit

I just accept it
I just watch it happen

as the blood runs through
her perfectly pale fingers

DESCENDING

These syllables
can't stop
me from the fall

but they make
the decent
all the more beautiful

PRECIPICE

I waited
at the precipice
for a thousand years
just so you could
push me over

and
now
I'm
smiling
all
the
way
down

FISHING IN THE VOID

O' abundance
O' beauty
he has squandered so much
Laid waste
to the kingdoms of pleasure
walking calmly from the flames
in the wake of abstinence
Such precision
within his destruction
Incalculable seasons
etched in the lines of his face
Beast and woman alike
sink to the history in his eyes
Such casual seduction
is not meant for one man
His love is broken -
in every shattered piece
is a sad song
the loneliness
of all astronauts

He could spend his life with you
and you would never touch his heart

THE SIREN

She blows me
a kiss
from the end of
love's synthesis

It burns through the night
in vapor waves
a contract so deep
it makes us both slaves

She shows me
fangs of bliss
that glow as they sink
into tragedy abyss

This is
casino lust
extinction
or bust

Intoxicated mad
laughter is our death dance
architects of Eden
purity stands no chance

Sin runs
like demonic oil
down the thighs
of a mortal coil

meticulous horror
in our bated breath
her seduction
more potent than death

Strict attention
is all her body craved
all ye who enter
become depraved

The moon refuses
her reflection
so she swallows it whole
rigor mortis erection

flesh is but more fuel
for the growing pyre
pulled apart with her
razor sharp desire

Her pheromone machine
commands the bones
The blood sings
as the sirens moans

BEAUTIFUL EXECUTIONERS

I met her at the bar
at the edge of the world
I wasn't looking for anything special
she was hoping for something different

Her mind was a slot machine
Our hearts just rigged casinos
At the precipice we drank away our reservations
We laughed our circumstance into the void

With every passing second we took our chances
Knowing full-well the fated outcomes
We rolled our dice and
commanded love into extinction

RAIN DANCE

She reminds me
of the actresses
in all the old movies
smoking cigarettes
relentlessly

So casual
Kool and easy –
And all at once
just as dangerous
and addictive

She was as free as
the day was long
holding captive
a man's highest curiosities

She danced even the longest nights
into grains of dust
She melted away the pain
with the rain that it brought

UNSEEN

She quells the fire in my chest
into a single quiet flame
but now that she's gone
it rages a trillion-fold
I am no longer a man
but a beast with
unseen horns and
a hell of an appetite

THE SPECTER

She has arrived once more
like a mystical apparition

she appears and instantly
I am brought to painful climax

all my sharp edges ooze
melting from advancing heartache

all the stars in my eyes explode
with the insanity of love's failure

She is a hollow-point bullet
I am a weak and limping target

She is the apocalypse
I am the walking dead

She is a knife
and I am useless meat

CAVED-IN

All my histories are
funneling toward her elegance

The walls of my heart
are being remodeled by her touch

My pride crumbling away
as her laughter shakes my ridged frame

Her body is an endless temple
and I am its solitary occupant

Mad with lust
and rabid with passion

I frantically search and destroy
every exit I can find

I just want to seal myself inside
this immaculate tomb forever

ADDICTED TO AN ILLUSION

Addicted to the illusion
that the days are passing
in the direction our minds are focused

Strung out and strung between neurons
like ghost ships in
foggy waters

Firing without a captain
lost to the whim of the storm's
malicious gaze

Our thoughts are born
blindfolded and
forced to walk the plank

You are free
to let go

You are free
to surrender

You are free
only not to be

GHOST KING

On these nights
still as frozen amber

I do everything in my power
to not remember her

to stifle the wild dream
but alas

the mind is a traitor
the heart is a ruin

And I am but the ghost
of a dead king

wandering this wasteland
haunting a once mighty empire

JUST A PHASE

She is the origin
& the destroyer
of all my worlds

She is the source
& the satisfaction
of all my hunger

She is the moon
& I am but the wax
and wane of her faces

NO REFUNDS

She was
the sensational poster
for a complete
disaster of a film

PARADOX OF CIRCUMSTANCE

We can never truly understand
how deep these roots go
until they are extracted
from their irreplaceable niche
in which event -
they can never return

THE UGLY TRUTH

Hope
is just
the makeup
on the
face of
reality

SILVER AND BLOOD

Strolling through the darkness
in a city so heartless

I pull my body's mass
through broken stained-glass

just to see that subtle curl
of her soft lips and white pearl

Hidden in all that misery
was a beautiful little victory

I died a thousand times
just to know her love was not a crime

seduced by her erratic pulsing
trapped in her constant convulsing

I was drawn like quicksilver
from her blood red river

I've never felt more alive
the hell I have survived

Love is so much sweeter
on death's tongue we teeter

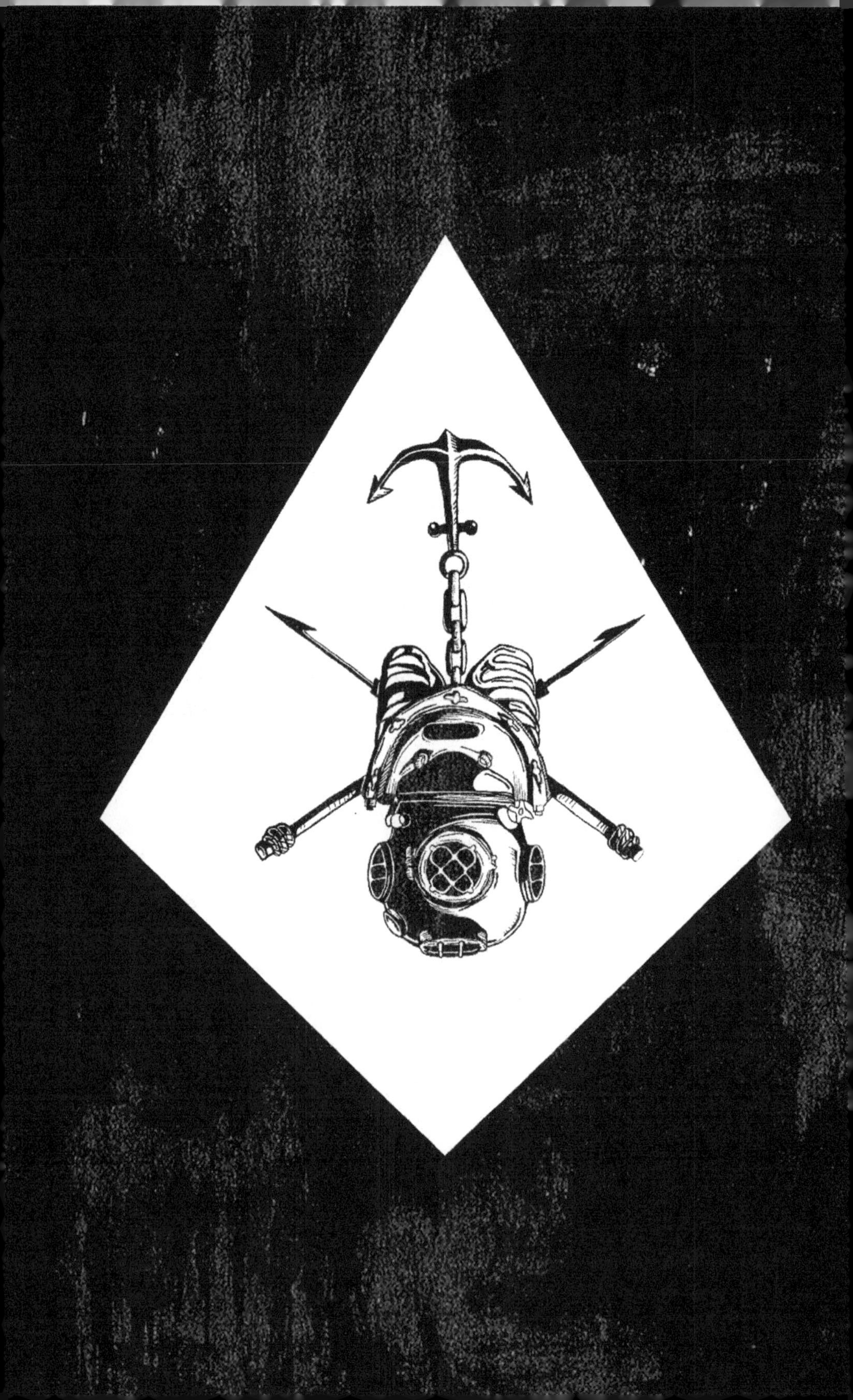

THE HOPELESS DIVER

How deep does the damn thing go?
We're swimming down
just to find out

We're dedicated
to pushing our way
to absolute bottom

There's a treasure down there
waiting to be held
lonely and pure

But the crux of it all
the irony in trying is -
we can never bring it to the surface

We can't drown
inside our dreams
but we can feel the horror

We can't fight the dead
and we can't know their peace
until we have become them

We are the greatest of contortionists
squeezing through
the tiniest of keyholes

only to realize
we've left what we came for
on the other side

THE ARCHAEOLOGIST

You think you see diamonds
in the smoldering embers
of the fire

You see some victory
in the broken remains
of human ruins

You still wander the wasteland
when there is nothing
left to scavenge

You look for meaning in pure madness
and don't find it funny
when it won't stop laughing

The taxidermic heart
no longer beats

The fallen monuments
no longer hold power

The blackened scrolls
give no knowledge

You are but a historian -
guessing at what might have been
you are just a desperate archeologist -
polishing ancient pain

ROMANTIC BLOODBATH

This is romantic bloodbath
This is lust gone insane

Hunger never satisfied –
no matter the feast

Our hearts are colliding
like blackholes

All of time collapsed
two pinpoint eyes

Crushed by the gravity
of this love

This is a heroic dose
in every hit

As drunk as a heathen god
on holiday

This intoxication
is life itself

EMPTY FORTRESS

Her heart was a fortress
a bastion of doubt

Her mind was a turret
a watchtower of anxious dreams

I was a swarm of mad children
flooding the castle gate

she inspired me to keep trying
No matter how hopeless it seemed

I got everything I needed in a word
in a slip of her tongue

whispers caught in the wind
grains of sand drifting in the ocean

Just beyond the impossible
is the chance I needed

In every game of roulette
with her sunken eyes

I was the most alive
I had ever realized

CHAINSAW LUST

She cuts through
every wall of my mind
with a chainsaw lust

She is the minotaur
lost in my maze
haunting every corner

her body
just a calculated
battle-axe

The sweetest of her words
drains the light
from the day

just like the
vampire
and its prey

The beautiful thing
has poison
on its lips!

Resurrection
is a curse
when death was a gift

THE METHOD

You
must
eat
hell
by the
mouthful
if you
want to
burn like
poetry

You must
never
tame the
hounds
guarding
your hell
if you
want
to keep
love
alive

LOGIC OF DOOMED SHIPS

An ancient skeleton is buried under layers of modern art
A skull is laughing at the absurd vehicle that it occupies

A mind is drowning in an ever-thickening ocean of blood
Boiling from overuse - running in every direction at once

Fear manifests in shadow and shapeless forms
Our choices move like marbles rolling down carved paths

Sinking ever deeper into a bed made of delicate vices
Slowly drifting off into longer and longer hibernations

A cold wind blows unto the last remaining embers
Teeth clench and chatter as a million tiny waves unite

There is only a moment to reflect upon an infinite void
There is but a fraction of a universe left to be curious

Worship what you will –
but the stars can't understand you

Pray if you must –
but make it sure it's in I's and O's

SLOW KILLER

She is a stack of dynamite
with a trillion tiny fuses

I am uncontrolled fire
growing ever more wild

She is a mad sun
swelling ever brighter

I am a small dark room
getting smaller by the second

She is a slow killer
and I don't know how to prey

A F T E R F L O W

She knows how
to bend the moans
like music notes

She plays
the nights
like a sad violin

All the while
a ceaseless
crescendo

Even when
the morning comes
and the music passes on

The tune
of her love
still hums in my mind

DEAD FLOWERS

She is but a bouquet
of dried up flowers
I keep in a beautiful vase
long past
their expiration date

She is all my
wilting memories
starving for
a drop of water
that will never come

I am the creep
who can't stop staring
wishing he could
paint life
back into her petals

BEHIND DREAM #1

Trapped in a room
with hundreds of doors
behind everyone - someone knocking

each time I reach for a handle
it detaches and falls away
useless and mocking

as I approach the last one
I hear a loud click
the sound of a permanent locking

THE PAIN OF BEAUTY

Cut this rope
sever this hope
still wrapped
around my neck

It keeps pulling
evermore -
but my heart
never stops

I'd rather fall
into the darkness below
than swing in limbo
staring at the angels -
forevermore

BLUE MOON

Once in awhile
her mystique
will bare its teeth
- the truth bleeds out

Once in awhile
her mystery
will shred me to pieces
- love like a dog

Every once in awhile
I get exactly
what I came for
- a new wound to lick

REFASHION

We are marching
through the sludge
of humanity
for a morsel of truth

We are on a pilgrimage
from rage
to the valley
of love

We are refashioning
all our weapons
into the tools
for a better world

FUCK OF DEATH

It was
the kiss of death
but damned if
she stopped there
she kept kissing
and then she started
sucking
draining
extracting
It's more accurate
to say
It was the full fuck of death
But it didn't kill me
It only brought me
back to life

REGARDLESS

To let passion in
is to risk it all

To understand dice and still play
is an act of true masochism

To love
is to die

As the words escape my mouth
I know we are doomed

In every kiss -
an execution

Hold me as tight as you possibly can -
because we are proof baby

that the universe can't stand
to love itself even one moment longer

TRADED MY PINS FOR YOUR NEEDLES

The pain from years of solitude
thaws from my face
replaced by your
crazed hex
absorbed into your
delirious sex
My path to you has been
a torturous crawl
My body feels
ragged and exhausted
My heart is screaming
from the bottom of a dark well
I beseech you my fertile captor
to throw down your barbarous hair
so I may fashion a rope
and sleep as the ancients do
Still echoing their song in the gallows
Now just softly swinging shadows

INCINERATED

O! the glory of her sun

She is the blooming
of every flower
in the depths
of all my winters

She is a light
brighter than
the very flame
she dances within

Her touch is
inescapable ecstasy
On the tip of her tongue
impossible passion

I bend
I fall
I writhe
I howl

I can only become
what she
needs me
to become

I can only be
incinerated
to briefly feed
the fire in her eyes

COVENANT IN THE MIRROR

An answer is down there
at the bottom of the sea
but you can never bring it to the surface

There is bliss way out there
in the furthest reaches of outer space
but all you know and understand
will be gone upon your return

To live - is to stare into a shattered mirror

GRIMOIRE

Her body is my grimoire
I am bound to her pages
written in crimson blood
encased in porcelain skin

Her mind is my labyrinth
there is no telling if I shall ever escape
wandering endlessly
lost in polychrome ecstasy

Her kiss is my hemlock
with every taste a bit closer to death
But with every new dawn
comes another chance to burn

MAXIMIZE THE ART

Each drop of you
is a canyon
I get lost in everyone

nights with you
pass
like a fever

the pleasure
always through
clenched teeth

We thread
moments
into our flesh

like we're reattaching
angel's wings
into our backs

We strengthen
our death machines
to maximize the art - of our dying

TAXIDERMY

Don't worry baby -
I won't dissect you this time
I won't analyze the pieces

This time around the sun
I'll just throw your body
strait into the river of time

But we both know that's not true
I've already stuffed you full of my desires
And now you're mounted
on every wall of my heart

WRAITHS

Upside down crosses
point to wicked exits

Long gone
but never quite dead

Beyond human
yet descended from beast

Bio-mechanical
flesh-trap Hell

There are far worse things
than Death herself

I call upon these wraiths
with a romantic suicide kiss

SPIRITUAL FERTILIZER

swimming effortlessly within
an ocean of chemical reactions

riding brunette waves
diving into crimson depths

this night is amaranthine bliss
this moment is an eternal kiss

she is a spiritual fertilizer
love's perfect crystallizer

she extends my seasons
and I bloom out of control

SADNESS WITHOUT A HOME

Meet me
in the middle
of forever

Don't stop now
we're almost halfway
to infinity

Depression
has laid a bitter kiss
on all of our joy

The brightest light
caught at the bottom
of the deepest sea

Our hearts beating
so furious
like exploding stars

Death is just the exhale
in the lungs of a universe
on fire

This dance never lasts long
but if we're lucky
it will light up the sky

GODLESS

My heart is *Death Valley*
My eyes are the windows to nothing

My hands caress the words
out from cold stones

I transfuse the blood from my body
until it is has all but vanished

Peace through
absolute zero

A stranger to existence
A darkness so deep it cannot be seen

Tempt not the desperate man
for you shall be punished

but worse yet is to notice the vacant one
for in his loneliness you shall be vanquished

TO COVER HER CANVAS

She is a feast for my eyes
yet no matter how long I stare
I am never full

My eyes need more teeth
to masticate her beauty
I chew but never swallow

She is the brightest flower
I am the bumbling bee
intoxicated mad by the nectar

My heart needs more blood
to cover her canvas
It is never enough

She is my plentiful garden
I am the worn out farmer
sewing his last seed

My hands are filthy
with death and
her dirt

PREY TO THE GODDESS

Her name was spontaneity
and her beauty was an explosion -
she painted my walls in red neon lust

Her heart was feral
rabid and running wild -
set loose upon my bedroom

Her hips shook
deeper than a sub-woofer-
an ass that broke worlds

She took my nights by storm
holding our bodies hostage
to infinite imaginations

A sexual serpent
in the most exquisite
feminine form

she slithered and sank
down into
the carpet threads

At times like these
it's wise to know your place
in the food chain

And like the good prey
I knew I was becoming -
I obeyed my nature

I only asked
that she took her
time with me

RUSTED ANCHORS

From my depths
to your sunken treasure
From my blade
to your quivering lips

This we cannot fathom
This we will never touch

More ink
to tell the tale
More blood
to give it color

From my tongue
to your hidden oasis
From my hollow
to your laughing fountain

This we cannot grasp
This will never last

More tears
to stain the pages
More wine
to drown out the ages

PLANNED

Forever strapped
to the chaos
of a chameleon
lust

This heart beats
to broken clocks
It will never
be the same

All music
has escaped
from the
beautiful machine

And now it rattles and shakes
kicking and squealing
no melody
no love

just the terrible noise
of an engine
becoming
obsolete

FOOD OF THE GODS

It's not perfection
they are after
They want the pain
built right into you

They want the knots
of anguish
placed neatly in a row

There is no value in
your purity
The virginity must be
cultivated with
notes of despair

They want a fine patina
of injury
in your human flesh

A potpourri of
survival wounds

You see - it's not what
you thought it was
When you fight
it gives them pleasure
The harder the better

The most brave
thrash and writhe
with immortal blood

It is these specimens
that will illuminate
the walls of Death's Heart

BEDROOM PANTHEON

These sheets are palimpsest with bittersweet memories
the walls still howling with a fertile vibration

written - overwritten
bitten by the hound
of damnation

How can we escape this total extinction?
the reason for our existence a fading infatuation

shattered - crushed
pulverized by lust
to dust

There are gods that have been killed for less
than what we went through this night

ejaculations - desolations
resurrection is the trap
of all temptations

CONJURE

These words are potions
This teypewriter is a laboratory
where alchemy becomes reality
We are able
to capture the essence -
manipulate its design

Submit chimeras
to extreme frontiers
the makers of new creatures

The bender of elements
to harness
novel experience

Sorcery to some
and just a gig to others
the science of the heart

Beware the mercury!
how it shifts and seduces
the untrained eye

The path that leads to knowledge
will erases its past
The ink that makes us mighty
will kill the mightiest

POISONED APPLES

The apocalypse never tasted better
washing it down with ripe intoxication

Watching the neon devils dance
with angels in their claws

short skirts and clipped wings
the poison gets us high!

We've become immune
to heaven's light

So pass another poison apple
and let's walk into the fire

You can no longer tempt
that which has gone insane

The blood of human hearts
the only paint left

spread upon
the decaying canvas of life

In a single moment
I shall show you a masterpiece

FAST HORSES / SLOW DAYS

nothing quite like a fresh hair-cut
on a hot day at the race track
with a great friend
and steady supply of alcoholic beverages

discussing strategies
of how to capture chaos in a jar
suspending logic
and putting common sense to sleep

because today we are riding the back
of a strange and majestic creature
where we land is not our choice
nor do we give a damn

You can have nothing or
you can have everything
it doesn't matter what you decide
the odds are always the same

NIGHTMARE KNOTS

No man escapes
from the nightmare knots -
her lips weave
into the fabric of
spontaneous nights

There is only surrender
There is only lust bursting
from inadequate cages

Her overpowered sexuality
collects every resistance
and folds them neatly
into a never ending chain
of broken hearts

She is some goddess
of chaos fertility
She's a Juggernaut of love!

Her fingers wrap so easily
around the largest of men
and squeeze out their rage
like a single candle flame
in the center of a blackhole

THE RISE AND FALL OF NOTHING HOLY

Every day
A rise - A chance - A way
Each night
A fall - A change - A death

These are but the masks we wear
The true face beneath - we cannot bear

Drawn down upon bloody knees
We dig up graves and ancient trees

Revealing ourselves and an empty past
In vile coffins - unified in a dirt caste

Where all our bodies are to be buried
there in the deepest sea - finally ferried

Tempted eternally with the love of Persephone
A war without end - cursed to be so in love

Swallowed by the fates in one enormous mouth
There is but one direction here
never north - forever southbound

ACCEPTANCE

You couldn't pay me to live your life
The freedom you claim comes at the price of too much guilt
not to mention the wagon full of fear
Your security unrecognizable from a prison cell
I see the vultures circling with their starving - hollow guts
I feel the jackals closing in - laughing at the nonsense in
their heads
I know no exit
I claim no paradise
But I do know when they come to take me away
I'll have become the devil they feared
I'll be the hell they've been praying about all the while

<u>SEVERED</u>

I avoid you like the plague -
ironically you hold the cure

You are a skeleton key -
unlocking every door of my heart

my hands - they shake too much
they can never find the hole

I understand myself -
only by exploring your landscapes

I remain empty -
until you fill me

You are so calm and patient -
watching me like an experiment

I am just a maniac -
who speaks in severed tongues

You are so indifferent -
I care far too much

FAUX

these words of passion
are spoken with fiery conviction
but they are but cold embers
unable to start anew

Just clever verses
manufactured like luxurious toy swords
but they are weak and faulty -
they cut nothing

Such warriors in the mind
mad-kings behind digital screens
yet upon examination
easily folded like paper soldiers

A brilliant display
of blooming feathers
washed flat
as the storm arrives

all those painted hues
drained from vacuous egos
and back into
abysmal palates

waiting always
for the canvas
that can truly hold
their color

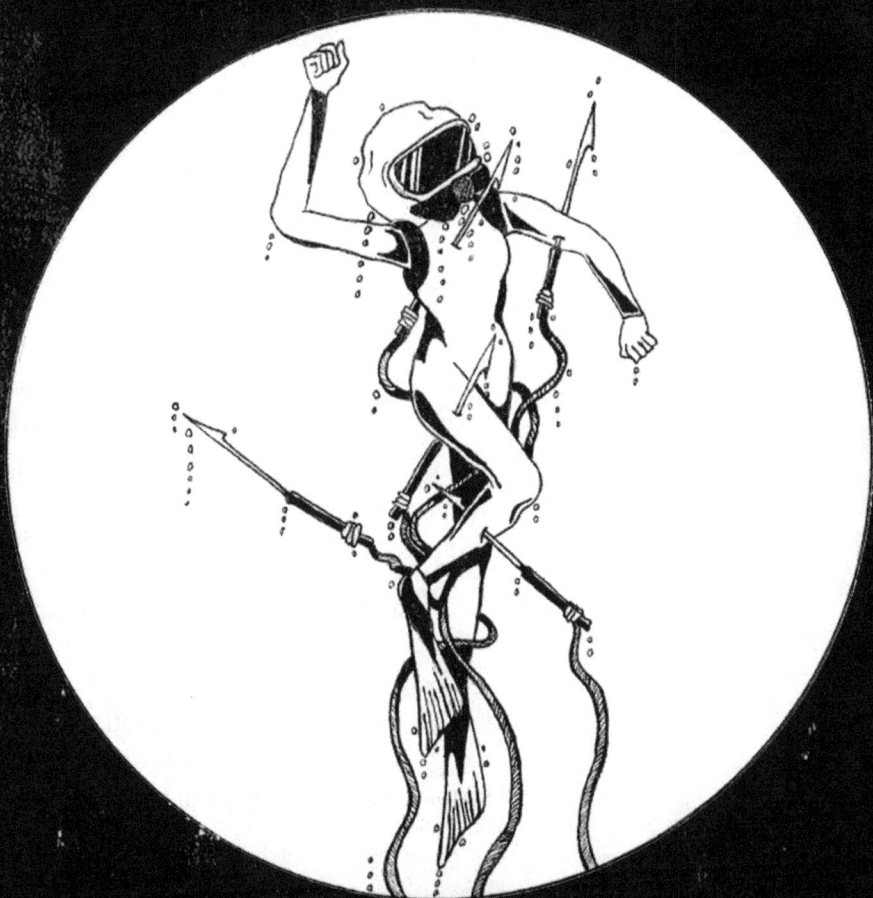

LUST AT SEA

Soft violence erupts -
shaking the sheets
and
injuring the silence

Soft violence wounds -
our tender flesh
and all these
dancing moments

softer
and softer -
yet all the more
extreme

Desire is a death race
with no end in sight
Desire has no outer-space
beyond this light

only a growing
demand
only a desperate
release

lust at sea
with a mad captain
drunk
at the helm

lust at sea
with endless spirits
consuming
our hearts

lust at sea
with no destination
yet a terrible treasure
pulling us downward

CHEERS TO THE FALLEN

We're on a ship
without a captain
heading full speed
toward the world's end

We are a compass
without a needle
spinning forever down
to the hell we have created

We're at war
without a reason
every battle fought
drunk off the chaos

We're truly lost
inside the nothingness
thinking that the next time
we question the stars -
they might actually answer

We are a full glass
of champagne
without a thing to celebrate
except our impending doom

JUST ANOTHER APOCALYPSE

There is a man at the end of the bar
with a brilliant idea
but he sure as hell
won't remember it in the morning

There is a woman at the opposite end of the same bar
with a simple wish
locked inside her heart
tonight she will lose the keys again

There are dreams floating
like dead bodies
in the remains of their drinks

Two desperate lovers
like melting ice cubes
so ephemeral and destined to disappear

"Would you choose a horse from the stables, traveler?"
asks the bartender

Sour - to mask the wounds
Spicy – to numb the conflict
Salty - to kill the hunger
Sweet - to forget death itself

AT THE BOTTOM

There's a poet
at the bottom of this book

You're a poet
if you're willing to die for it

There's always poetry
in the last little bit of it

Just hold on..
until it reappears

Summate all the losses
they have a new purpose now

colors are brighter -
when you're starving

The survivors feel it most -
they understand all too well

what's at the bottom -
of this

Hold tight-
just a little longer now

don't move -
just sink

stay strong -
don't breath...

BEWARE

My heart
is a junkyard dog
rapid with lust
wild for new love

These chains
are but trinkets
to the inevitable
escape

No wall
No gate
No collar
can hold back the hunger

No man
No mortal
No fool on fire
would dare deny my intent

Beware the sleeping beast
for when he awakes
his bite is far worse
than the hell he protects

BABY GO BOOM

There is a terrorist
between her legs
and I am just a victim

Hidden in rosy flesh
are weapons
of mass seduction

I'm nothing more
than a talking head
with no words to speak of

Just a silent solider
fighting for her
to surrender explosions

SLOW BURN

A woman's
eyes
are the most
dangerous
of all
man's
fires

BENEATH THE VEIL

Just beneath that veil
she keeps so tight around
her lips
is a doorway to
unbreakable nights
and further toward
hearts that beat in
unison
Her swagger and her sway
they evade
most all her suitors attempts
Her sinking eyes
and sultry hips
they intimidate as
they beckon

Few can muster the strength
it takes to give her
proper council
even fewer have attempted
to climb the walls
and see her kingdom
in full

She is terrified and alone
imbedded in all that beauty

Only a man with true intent
will save her from the
sadness

A man who is just crazy enough
one who needs her
to cure his own
madness

SWALLOWED

Rather be swept along in this chaos and mystery
then cemented in the trap of their platitudes

Rather be disassembled for any useful parts
than thrown in their scrapheap of wasted love

O' they have forgotten that love is found not pleaded for
A million kisses from the wrong lips will only decay the heart

O' how these men have become so abandoned!
Nothing remains - only a barren lust in a hollow place

An unforgiving wind drives the fertility from their bones
Only the abyss can be impregnated now

For the sake of mankind and the chance of future innocence
I hope she can keep down all that she has swallowed

AFTER THE LAST DROP

An empty man
walks down
an empty street
drinking from
empty bottles
thinking about
how many different ways
he can write about
nothing at all
and still survive

EDGE

The edge of the world
is on the tip of my tongue

When we kiss
we fall forever
Pucker up baby!

HARD LUCK

woman
and
horses

the odds are
always
the same -

yet we still bet
till our pockets
run dry

BLACK-CHERRY LEMONADE

When words won't due
but the kiss says it all

When you would trade every line of dialogue
for the single sex scene

A few fists full of her dark hair
give me all the reason I will ever need

Our tongues and teeth
dig into flesh to finding release

Our hands surprisingly fluent
in each-other's foreign bodies

Bending to express our intent
our shifting silhouettes

make beautiful creatures
on vaulted ceilings

With every second - a silent NO
and a million yes yes yes

flavored booze washes down
the imperfections of our creation
Our bodies wash each other
in sweat we become clean
The past is murdered
by the beauty of our present
Our pain dissolves into the air
with each desperate moan

The impossible weight of our circumstance
thrown effortlessly into this night's abyss

THE LOST SAILOR

I am a lost sailor here
deserted for years upon years

I contemplate the vacancy of my ship
Drunk off the madness of my blight

Hunger - is the most honest beauty
starvation is salvation
I am a stowaway within myself
hanged and haunted

There is a row of black sails
far off out on the crest of the horizon

I am incessantly driven toward
the promise of my destruction
because it is the only escape
from a hollow love

The blue waters themselves
drowning in a thick darkness of uncertainty
Directions matter little when
you've been spun around this many times
my heart like a rogue planet in chaos orbit
flung wildly into uncharted space

I am both full of terror
and blissfully serene

If I could only hear your voice
If I could just catch a glimmer

Determination is the dullest of knives
when you consider what it's cutting

SMALL BUT ACCUMULATING CUTS

How cryptic -
How obscure -
shouldn't we talk about it?
before we no longer understand the meaning?
before we can't see each other at all?

I'm a spy
and you're a spy too
You double crossed my under-the-covers attack
I'm in love with you - not loving the me I thought you
thought I was
You're infatuated with me - not loving the you that you
can't stand to be

How cryptic...
How obscure...
Should we talk about it?
before we end up right where we started?
before we forget what it was all about?

There are no shortcuts through this Hell
And there is no cheating in this Love
We are stray bullets aimed at each-others hearts
if they both land then we both get what neither of us can
stand
if they both miss we might just feel our last kiss - again

How cryptic...
How obscure...
How much damage can we take
before it doesn't hurt at all?
How many secrets can we tell ourselves -
so that we believe the one we never could?

PLAYING IMPOSSIBLE TO GET

She doesn't want me
because I want her
She don't need a man
she just wants someone
who can "understand"
And she can't stand
the ones that press the issue
yet she loves the ones
who answer when she calls
She thinks it's annoying
when they call too much
when they want it so bad
She wants it when she wants it
not before - not after
little miss goldilocks
When I'm foaming at the mouth
and she's too busy acting coy
When I'm the Big Bad on the hunt
and she's just the innocent victim
O' me O' my
But then
when she gets the taste
a passing whim
O' that queen gets
what that queen desires
We all give in to her game -
don't we?
She watches it on TV
She reads it in the novels
She dreams a little wet dream
All that passion
and insatiable obsession
it gets her ripe

it turns her on
but when I arrive
with the real thing
she casually tosses it aside
She don't want
what she think she wants
But god damn it if
I don't know
exactly what I need

MAZEMIND

My mind has become like
a maze with no exits

Only long stretches
of terminals playing charades

A taunting logic
dances in the shadows

a mathematical Cheshire Cat
(whispering of new ways out)

a solution glitters
in my peripheries

like a shifting oasis
under a golden sun

running as fast as I can
through the days and tasks

subconscious suggestions
only accelerate my madness

standing still is like being
pulled apart from the inside

War is fought
in every breath

Death cannot be found
and love is impossible

The slow withering of this beauty
The glorious efficiency of decay

I must remember to surrender
I must let go of everything

The only choice is to give in
for I cannot leave here

I can only attempt to understand
the poetry of the maze

D I M

dim days bending strange
the mind slips away and
forgets itself -
the mystery of memory

tiny beasts sinking deep
imbedding
in crystal skulls -
pretty niches

sucking and taking
there's nothing left
for the broken sunlight -
fallow fields

vampires of indecision
bottomless bellies
draining smiles -
teeter extinction

wishing for brighter days
salt to gaping wounds
laughing is foreign -
madness's gift

the pain of other's pleasures
all it would take
is to move one finger -
graveyard voices

trivial requests
feet locked in
in carpet circles -
slow spirals

a brain like an old
warped record
filled with empty choices -
infinity reach

torturous are the hours
options bound in fear
balled up and black -
waiting to implode

THE HARD GOODBYE

An unexpected dance
with an old friend
A wish on her tongue
The kiss of death soon to follow
I had to wear my sunglasses indoors
or else her body's hellfire
would have melted my irises
I grabbed the bottle of Vicodins
like a hand grenade
washed a few down with neon green
Absinthe gives even the weakest of men
the courage to reach into the darkness
and retrieve his muddy heart For you see -
Goodbyes can take forever
especially when your tongues are tied
in knots and nooses
Goodbyes can last forever
when your hands are at war
for dominance upon
fleshy landscapes Goodbyes can be tantric
when your curiosities
are never questioned
only reciprocated and advanced
when your desires are accelerating
your perversions growing wild
Goodbyes can wrap themselves
around your skull
They can be as soft as
the inside of a ripe peach
yet as deadly
as drinking pure bleach
They can tear your ego apart
and bury all the pieces
right between
the legs of an angel

THE FLY

I've arrived once again

without warning -
tossed into
a limbo of
chemical indecision

outside -
tiny universes
bursting and blooming
with the colors of creation

inside -
the promise of death
silence in a cage
of lonely thoughts

doorways like trapdoors
leading back to the center
Exits like false prophets
that lie to get their way

crippled by
a head full of options
unable to decide -
rotting heart

subatomic forces
parade the skull
closing each window
just as soon as it appears

pounds of caffeine
paradoxically induce sleep
minutes pass like lovers
into a swelling graveyard

sex only exists on a computer screen
nature is just a program
laughter is a simulation
echoing

caught within a spider's inner-web
weaved from long nightmares
hypnotized by The Nothing
the trance is the dance

and when I finally escape
the sun has always disappeared

CIRCUS

They're handing out new prescriptions to match our every mood.
But they must manufacture more moods to sell us ever more pills.
Can someone please show me the exit to this haunted house stuffed with ghosts? I'm lost in all these options.
Behind ever door is just the same clown with new makeup.
I'm telling you man, you've got to have real guts to make a stand in this world.
It's a circus of opinions and it's right outside the door.
Facts are just magic tricks.
Truth is a fog machine.
Everyone seems to be the center of a universe.
The streets are getting crowded with bankrupt minds.
Obese and begging for justice.
Bartering violence for personal truths and misinformation.
It's the trained glimmer in their eyes.
It's the quick spin on their tongues.
What will they try and sell us next?
World peace through organic crystal meditation?
The end of all hate by addressing everyone by the proper pronoun, just to say hello?
The perfect diet. A fool proof financial strategy. A lifetime warranty.
Offending someone these days might as well be murder in the first degree.
And god forbid you tell a beautiful woman anything but the time.
It just might ruin your life.
Once upon a time you could fart on a church pew.
One loud enough to make the crucifix shake and they would still forgive you.
Now you'd be locked up as a religious terrorist.
Does anyone feel like we've become social bubble-boys?
Responding to our own voices echoing off plastic surfaces.

Sterilizing even the slightest possibility of a controversial idea.
Beware "cross-contamination." Fear all evolution. Praise dead revolutions.
Just a mob inside mob, deepening our isolations.
The bully is in every word. The lie is every headline.
True terror is a child's homemade clock.
The rapist is any man with eyes.
The heinous pervert is a guy just over 35
years old, sitting at the bar hoping to get laid.
Censorship at all costs. Cover the children eyes.
Watch it later on T.V.
Worship the guns. Desensitize the blood.
Veil the sex with black boxes. Criminalize all the drugs.
Editing our consciousness to sell more doubt.
They push salvation from a hell they created.
Their god is fear made flesh.
They must first name it, so they can destroy it.
It's all just according to protocol.
Convince the masses it's unnatural, wicked, and danger-ous.
Then incarcerate or exterminate.
I'm running in circles looking for a hole in the Big Top.
And when I do, I'm crawling out, with my damned guts intact.

MULTIPLES

There was the one with hair like Rapunzel
stretched for miles over my skin
she would wrap me in her black widow's web
spin me tightly into her heartache
I was prey and yet I prayed to never leave
that cocoon of twisted delight

There was the one with the heavenly body
her hips were sexual violence
once caught in their gravity
you could do nothing but go along for the ride
She was like Saturn with those glorious rings
spinning us both so flat against fate

There was the one with the mouth of Aphrodite
she giveth and oh could she taketh away
she contained within her such power
all the fire of Hell and the promise of paradise
an oasis of pleasure in the desert of pain
I would gladly trade my life to drown in her fountains

There was one for each one of me
One simple version for all my multiplicity

MAGICIANS

There are magicians that walk amongst us
encrypted in their genetics are incantations
able to seduce the hordes, marionette the masses
Some pre-flood technology written in the code
You look at them and they look straight through you
Enraptured by their power, all we can do is say yes
We feel the touch of divinity when our skins collide
We become like some intoxicated pet
obeying just to receive their affection, holy attention

There are necromancers that live all around us
embedded in their biology is a higher design
able to resurrect the idea of man or
refashion a woman's heart
Some high tech ancient knowledge burning in their heads
You look at them and they look at what you could become
Exhausted by their spiritual gravity we can only give in
We feel the persuasive kiss of death when our souls engage
We drown in the sea of mutant kind
and we are lifted from those dark waters, as a willing
sacrifice

EAGER DICE

Sometimes you just know
 exactly when to strike
You know that if you choke
 it's all over
no debate
no redoes
no some other time
you just got to do it -
what the moment demands
You are a solider of luck now kid
and the dice don't roll themselves
and when you finally feel it
the air will be so crisp
an invisible wave will
crash over all your fears
Some tough Motherfucker
inside you
will start telling you exactly what to do
and you will do it
See that pretty gal over there?
Yeah that's the one doofus
You're going to turn into Romeo
Poof!
like right now
and then you're going to walk on over there
and show that beautiful young Juliet
one hell of a good time
Did you hear me?
And just like that -
like the good solider you are
you do as you're told

If you can make Fortune smile
that's usually a good start

CULT OF BUKOWSKI

The cult of Bukowski
is growing weak -
going extinct

They've lost their way
Full of mushy egos
that "expect" things

Worse yet
begging for handouts
and petty attention

A circle jerks
of care-bears
relentlessly chanting
"we care we care"

He tried to tell us
it's all going to be ok -
if we just stay drunk
but did they listen?

Now they just
whisper sweet nothings
into each-others skulls

constantly reminding
one another that
every flaw is some kind of perfection...
that we're all super special
"in our own way"

Now they only buy self-help books
It's Hardcore masturbation
everywhere you turn

holding on tight
to the illusion of
perpetual progress

The words no longer
mean a thing you see -
"chaos" is just a cool word for sexy

The greatest chaos they can understand
is but an anxious puppy -
teething on their new slippers
They sell themselves
one LIEners
expecting to get rich

They want payment in full
from one day's worth
of pain

Our hero
is now a cheap tattoo
an overpriced pop icon poster

they have cherry picked
the valley
and ran away

The realest poetry
is still rotting
on the vine

JUST ANOTHER SHITTY LOVE POEM

Does she really understand
how often I think about tasting her flesh?

Not just casually viewing the flower
but rather - full emersion

No, it's not just any flower – It's Divine!
O' the army I've become
just to get inside her walls

The killer I become
to defend her smile

The wreck I am
when she cuts me from her light

Will she ever come to grips
with how fascinated I really am?

I worship her like a desert oasis
Only her touch can heal me

Her lips the master
enslaving me with every kiss

I am an ancient forest -
tired of my own existence
She is the burning wild

She is the light of resurrection
I am the filth of the past

She washes over all of me
cleansing me to extinction

Does she even realize -
I only live to die inside her?

THE SINKING SKYLINE

Tracing the skyline
with a delicate finger
because you know
this must collapse

Observing the lights
flickering in and out of existence
because you know
this cannot last

Nostalgia is the hungriest
of our beasts
For it consumes every moment
just as soon as it arrives

Our eyes are fixated
on an impossible horizon
Our hearts firmly tied
to an ever-ticking clock

If you could only find the beauty
in the ugliest of things
Then you will have won yourself
a prize beyond comprehension

BRUISED NOT BROKEN

My heart is black and blue
from all the beatings
that I took from you

You were ruthless
You were so unforgiving
relentlessly vacant

Your beauty makes you cold
some faux prostitute
that never puts out

over priced
over the counter
over the edge

forever isolated
forever stone
such false devotion

I hope he breaks you
I hope he wears you down
Not for my satisfaction -
but for your own good

Every monster
should see its own
face reflected
.

So when the slayer finally comes
your destruction
will be accepted

And in that glorious wreckage
a hundred hearts restored

ANALYSIS IN THREE PARTS

I
savage barbarian
in a three-piece suit
I've taken everything
that puts a glimmer in my eye
I've tasted all her flavors
each and every shade
I am never full
I savor only the moment of
extinction
II
insane sailor
holding his crew captive
An audience to love gone mad
By the end of this voyage
We will all walk the plank!
The rum is long gone -
we sail only to find more sea
Each wave
as wild as the last
our sins
the proof of our past
III
amnesic fiend
on a never-ending hunt
I've had everything I need
and I destroy it in turn
I recycle emotions like
water on a turning wheel
One replacing the other
I watch as the patterns repeat
But I remember nothing
I cannot hold on
yet I cannot let go

A MAZE TOO SWEET

There I was
leaning casually
against the day
gin & tonics
sliding urgently toward
some final destination

She was a surprise gift
spontaneous like a Gatling-gun
pure and strong - a blazing sun
Her radiance was everywhere
bullets through a glass heart

There I was
a slob caught
with his head
up in the clouds
watching shadows
crawl across the earth
slow hours creeping toward
some hidden destination

She was a lioness
with a mane made of devilish light
with a tongue slipping pure delight
Her den was everywhere
she laid her bloody paws

There I went
wandering through
a soft garden
purging my lust
down halls of pleasure
A maze too sweet
to escape -
untouched or
untasted

MAKES THE HEART DECAY FONDER

I loved her tits -
because they never needed an audience
or a push-up bra

I loved her face - (pores and all)
it was intensely beautiful
without all the crude

I loved her mind -
for all its intricacies and contradictions
its spontaneous delights

I loved her wit -
it cut quick and sharp
the finest of switchblades

I loved her sarcasm -
wonderfully disarming
and O' so liberating

I loved her eyes -
when she was finally satisfied
they radiated such rare lights

I loved her touch -
when she wanted to be loved
inescapable trap

I loved her distance -
when she had had enough
severely complete

I even love the bitter aftertaste

SILENCER

Serpentine temptress
long blank extrinsic
strong and dangerous
lethal bliss
infectious paradise
years slide by like oiled flesh
slithering through caverns
of a bloody heart
wrapping tight
deep within the ribcage
the cycles completed
when a beautiful dark body
constricts and commands
in seductive power
No poison was spent
only a kiss delivered
A kiss so severe
no scream could escape
nor love be found

DETAILS OF THE PAIN

So you want the flood
because you think you can survive it

You think you got the guts
to crawl through this heartache

You call for the truth serum
because you want all the details

What street I was on -
when I caved in

The time of day it was -
when we destroyed love itself

The season
and the midnight mood

You want a logic
for an abstract heart
You wish to identify
with this pain

You feel a need to name
this psychosis
You want the temperature
of the flames at which I burned

The shape of the needle
that punctured the skin
of a vampire

You need solutions
to the chaos equation
of my mind

You want what I couldn't possibly give
and yet this story I relive

You want the map
to a growing wasteland

LOVE'S DANCE

Maybe it's because I was an only child for so long
Maybe it's all that television and video games
Maybe just maybe - it's genetic predisposition

The violence
I got it
it's wrapped up in my heart
It hides on the tip of my tongue
It's always there - coiled and whispering
building up its strength
If you aren't ready to fight for it
then what's it good for?
If you're not prepared to kill for it
(I'll ask once more)
What the hell's it good for?

The blood
it's important to see its depth
fresh from the source
deep like crimson moon
The sacrifice of pain
is the only way
to ever know
anything by its real name

Violence is just love
dancing
in its own blood

COMPLICIT

Knowing full well
the effects of her poison
I swallow her again and again
with all the terror of a newborn
but the resolve of a warrior

Understanding the risks
of her dangerous beauty
I dive into her depths
No vision to navigate
only the hope of a new species

She is a ritual
A path to the sun
I am feeble and blinded
and still I crawl
ceaselessly toward her light
I thirst to prove my desire

She is incendiary
an untamed power
I am an arrow
shot in the darkness
of her maze
I travel so strange
that I just might survive

Her tongue knows
the sound of all words
Her body is an ancient lock
I'm the untrained key
I will risk everything
to solve a piece of the puzzle

IN EXILE

Lust with
contradictions
Immortality dies

Ripe with
paradox
Death gives birth

This is poetry
in exile

Crystalline messages
from the outer spaces
of a deranged mind

Coded transmissions
from the depths
of a sunken soul

This poetry must remain
in exile

Bored in paradise
the angels
pluck their wings

Ecstatic in hell
the demons
fall in love

This is the poetry
of the exiled

DESCENDING MT. BLISS

beckoning
from strange heights
tugging from within
every tiny nook
calling
dragging towards
peak of possibility
limits of comprehension
crawling toward
inching ever near
resonating valency
expanding darkness
closer to the sirens
match the harmonies
bask in unknown beauties
the pulsing in every cell
So close
enchanted eyes
quivering lips
the smell of god
arriving at the mountaintop
climax
zenith of bliss
filled with the joy of creation
supernova
kaleidoscope of pleasure
lasting just long enough
to glimpse
the angel's smile turning
into the mouth of hell
ecstasy exchanged
with the dread
of infinite falling

INVERTED / PERVERTED

sink to the bottom
float to the top

flip me upside down
turn me inside out

float to the bottom
sink to the top

from the depths to the extreme
that's what it's all about

RAPTURE

curiosity is pregnant with obsession
the mother of pure intoxication
highs reaching for an edge
lows sinking below the earth

pushing out the perimeters of bliss
dredging the trenches of despair
there lies the most sacred
there sits the immovable core

reason dissolves before beauty
every risk - worth a glimpse
a life - for a lingering taste
to hold - but never keep

the return is a teetering choice
the amnesia is near certain
the treasure is a ghost
we hope haunts us forever